· TRIPLE TESTED ·
FOR YOUR SUCCESS EVERY TIME

From the moment you sift the flour, you can forget the mystique about making pastry. Following our step-by-step tips and techniques, you'll soon feel confident as you make the delicious pies, tarts, quiches and other surprises in this book. The pastries we used most often are grouped, starting on page 112, while others are given with individual recipes. Many recipes can be prepared ahead, and some use ready-rolled pastry for times when you're really in a rush.

Pamela Clark

FOOD EDITOR

pies and tarts

Pies and tarts...

Everybody loves a pie. In all its many guises, it's one of the most versatile of dishes, being as happy at an informal picnic as it is at a formal dinner. From a traditional family meat pie with the flakiest of crusts, to light-as-a-feather dessert tarts – here is a collection of recipes your family and guests will adore. If you think you couldn't possibly make decent pastry, prepare to be surprised: once you master the basic techniques, you'll wonder what all the fuss was about...

Apricot Bakewell Tart, page 99

Spiced Apricot and Plum Pie, page 76

Zucchini and Feta Spiral, page 44

Contents

Kidneys with Mustard and Capers in Fillo, page 38

BRITISH & NORTH AMERICAN READERS:
Please note that Australian cup and spoon measurements are
metric. A quick conversion guide appears on page 120.

Snacks and finger food

All the exciting little shapes and delectable tastes of these tempting savouries are fun at parties, as appetisers at dinner parties or any time finger food suits the occasion. We've included a classic selection of savoury treats including ratatouille palmiers, puffs, pies and a scrumptious variety of tartlets, all of which will ensure the success of your next celebration.

SCRAMBLED EGG AND SMOKED SALMON TARTLETS

Cut out tartlets in batches, re-rolling pastry as necessary.

1¹/₂ cups (225g) plain flour
125g cold butter, chopped
1 egg yolk
2 teaspoons chopped fresh basil
2 teaspoons chopped fresh dill
2 teaspoons chopped fresh chives
pinch cayenne pepper
3 teaspoons iced water, approximately
2 slices (50g) smoked salmon
1 tablespoon chopped fresh chives

SCRAMBLED EGGS
4 eggs, lightly beaten
1/4 cup (60ml) cream
2 teaspoons chopped fresh dill
20g butter

Grease 3 x 12-hole tartlet trays. Sift flour into bowl, rub in butter (or process flour and butter until mixture resembles breadcrumbs). Add egg yolk, herbs, pepper and enough water to make ingredients cling together (or process into a ball), knead gently on lightly floured surface until smooth. Wrap in plastic, refrigerate 30 minutes.

Roll pastry between sheets of baking paper until 2mm thick. Cut pastry into 36 x 6cm rounds, place rounds into prepared trays, lightly prick with fork, refrigerate 30 minutes. Bake in moderately hot oven 10 minutes. Press pastry cases carefully with the back of a spoon, bake further 10 minutes or until pastry is browned, cool.

Cut salmon into thin strips. Spoon scrambled eggs evenly into pastry cases, top with salmon and chives.

Scrambled Eggs Combine eggs, cream and dill in bowl, mix well. Heat butter in pan, add egg mixture, cook over low heat, stirring gently, until creamy and just set.

MAKES 36

Pastry cases can be made 5 days ahead. Scrambled eggs best made just before serving.

Opposite, from left Scrambled egg and smoked salmon tartlets; Smoked chicken and cheese puffs

Storage Airtight container
Freeze Pastry cases suitable
Microwave Scrambled eggs suitable

GOATS' CHEESE, OLIVE AND TOMATO TARTLETS

Cut out tartlets in batches, re-rolling pastry as necessary.

1¹/₂ cups (225g) plain flour
125g cold butter, chopped
¹/₄ cup (35g) finely chopped
   drained sun-dried tomatoes
1 egg yolk
1 tablespoon iced water,
   approximately
1 tablespoon chopped fresh parsley

FILLING
2 eggs
1 cup (250ml) cream
150g goats' cheese, chopped
¹/₂ small (40g) onion,
   finely chopped
¹/₄ medium (50g) red pepper,
   finely chopped
¹/₄ medium (50g) yellow pepper,
   finely chopped
8 seedless black olives,
   finely chopped
1 tablespoon chopped fresh thyme
1 tablespoon chopped fresh parsley

Grease 30 x 6cm square tartlet tins. Process flour, butter and tomatoes about 30 seconds or until mixture resembles breadcrumbs. Add egg yolk and enough water to make ingredients just cling together. Press dough into a ball, knead gently on floured surface until smooth. Wrap in plastic, refrigerate 30 minutes.

Roll pastry between sheets of baking paper until 1mm thick. Cut pastry into 7cm squares, lift squares into prepared tins, ease into sides, trim edges. Lightly prick bases with fork, place tins on oven trays, refrigerate 30 minutes.

Spoon level tablespoons of filling into pastry cases, smooth tops. Bake in hot oven about 25 minutes or until pastry is cooked and filling browned. Cool in tins. Serve sprinkled with parsley.

Filling Beat eggs, cream and cheese in small bowl with electric mixer until smooth. Stir in onion, peppers, olives, thyme and parsley.

MAKES 30

Recipe can be made a day ahead.

Storage Covered, in refrigerator
Freeze Cooked tartlets suitable
Microwave Not suitable

SMOKED CHICKEN AND CHEESE PUFFS

¹/₂ cup (125ml) water
40g butter, chopped
¹/₂ cup (75g) plain flour
1 teaspoon seasoned pepper
2 eggs, lightly beaten
¹/₂ cup (60g) finely grated
   smoked cheese
1 small (115g) skinless smoked
   chicken breast, finely chopped
vegetable oil for deep-frying

Combine water and butter in pan, bring to boil, stirring, until butter is melted. Add sifted flour and pepper all at once, stir vigorously over heat until mixture leaves side of pan and forms a smooth ball.

Transfer mixture to small bowl of electric mixer (or processor). Add eggs 1 at a time, beat on low speed until smooth after each addition. Stir in cheese and chicken; mix well.

Just before serving, deep-fry rounded teaspoons of mixture in hot oil until lightly browned and cooked through; drain on absorbent paper.

MAKES ABOUT 35

Mixture can be prepared an hour ahead.

Storage At room temperature
Freeze Not suitable
Microwave Not suitable

OLIVES IN CHEESE PASTRY

Cut out rounds in batches, re-rolling pastry as necessary.

50 (200g) pimiento-stuffed
   green olives
1 cup (150g) plain flour
pinch cayenne pepper
100g butter, chopped
1¹/₄ cups (155g) grated tasty
   cheddar cheese
1 egg, lightly beaten
2 tablespoons sesame seeds

Pat olives dry with absorbent paper. Process flour, pepper and butter until mixture resembles breadcrumbs. Add cheese, process until mixture forms a ball. Knead dough on floured surface until smooth; cover, refrigerate 30 minutes.

Roll pastry between sheets of baking paper until 3mm thick. Cut pastry into 50 x 4.5cm rounds, top each round with an olive, fold pastry around olives to enclose, roll into balls.

Dip tops of balls in egg, then seeds. Place balls onto greased oven tray; refrigerate 30 minutes.

Bake in moderately hot oven about 15 minutes or until lightly browned, cool.

MAKES 50

Recipe can be made a day ahead.

Storage Airtight container
Freeze Uncooked pastry suitable
Microwave Not suitable

Left, from top Goats' cheese, olive and tomato tartlets; Olives in cheese pastry
Right, from top Mini silverbeet and feta cheese pies; Mini potato and bacon pasties

MINI SILVERBEET AND FETA CHEESE PIES

6 sheets fillo pastry
60g butter, melted

FILLING
2 tablespoons olive oil
2 cloves garlic, crushed
6 green shallots, chopped
1 bunch (1kg) silverbeet, shredded
200g feta cheese, crumbled
200g ricotta cheese
1/4 teaspoon ground nutmeg
3 eggs, lightly beaten
2 tablespoons chopped fresh parsley
1/2 cup (35g) stale breadcrumbs

Grease 12-hole muffin pan (1/3 cup/80ml capacity). Brush 1 sheet of pastry with butter, fold in half crossways. Brush with

butter, cut into 4 squares. Layer 2 squares together at angles in 1 hole of prepared pan. Repeat with remaining squares, then remaining pastry and butter.

Spoon filling into pastry cases, fold pastry over to cover filling, brush with remaining butter. Bake in moderately hot oven about 15 minutes or until browned.

Filling Heat oil in pan, add garlic and shallots, cook, stirring, 1 minute. Add silverbeet, cook, stirring, until wilted, drain, cool. Squeeze excess liquid from silverbeet. Combine cheeses, nutmeg and eggs in bowl, mix well; stir in silverbeet mixture, parsley and breadcrumbs.

MAKES 12

Recipes can be made several hours ahead.

Storage Covered, in refrigerator
Freeze Not suitable
Microwave Silverbeet suitable

MINI POTATO AND BACON PASTIES

2 quantities basic shortcrust pastry; recipe page 112
1 egg yolk
2 tablespoons milk
1 1/2 teaspoons poppy seeds

FILLING
3 medium (600g) potatoes, chopped
1/2 cup (125ml) sour cream
1 tablespoon chopped fresh thyme
1 tablespoon chopped fresh chives
2 teaspoons seeded mustard
30g butter
1 small (80g) onion, chopped
2 cloves garlic, crushed
2 bacon rashers, chopped

Make pastry according to directions on page 112. Roll half the pastry between sheets of baking paper until 2mm thick. Cut pastry into 15 x 10cm rounds. Repeat with remaining pastry.

Place 1 level tablespoon of filling in centre of each round. Brush edges with combined egg yolk and milk, fold in half, press edges together to seal.

Place pastries on greased oven trays, brush with remaining milk mixture; sprinkle with seeds. Bake in moderately hot oven about 25 minutes or until pastry is lightly browned.

Filling Boil, steam or microwave potatoes until tender, cool 10 minutes. Combine potatoes, sour cream, herbs and mustard in bowl; mix well. Heat butter in pan, add onion, garlic and bacon, cook, stirring, until onion is soft. Add onion mixture to potato mixture; mix well.

MAKES 30

Pastries can be made a day ahead.

Storage Covered, in refrigerator
Freeze Cooked pasties suitable
Microwave Potatoes suitable

MAKES ABOUT 30
Pastry cases can be made a day ahead.

Storage Airtight container
Freeze Pastry cases suitable
Microwave Not suitable

BARBECUED PORK WITH PLUM GLAZE TARTLETS

Cut out tartlets in batches, re-rolling pastry as necessary.

1½ cups (225g) plain flour
125g cold butter, chopped
¼ cup (35g) sesame seeds, toasted
1 egg yolk
3 teaspoons iced water, approximately
250g barbecued pork, thinly sliced
2 tablespoons plum sauce
2 green shallots, sliced

FILLING
40g butter
2 medium (300g) onions, chopped
1 clove garlic, crushed
1 teaspoon grated fresh ginger
2 teaspoons cornflour
1 tablespoon water
2 teaspoons soy sauce
¼ cup (60ml) plum sauce
1 tablespoon dry sherry

BLUE CHEESE AND CELERIAC BITES

2 sheets ready-rolled puff pastry
1 egg, lightly beaten
½ cup fresh flat-leafed parsley leaves

FILLING
½ small (180g) celeriac, chopped
1 cup (250ml) cream
100g blue-vein cheese, chopped
1 cup (250ml) sour cream

Place pastry sheets on lightly floured surface. Brush lightly with egg. Cut pastry into 5cm rounds. Mark 3cm circle in centre of each round; do not cut all the way through. Place rounds on oven trays, bake in hot oven about 20 minutes or until pastry is browned and puffed. Cool on wire racks.

Press down inner circles with thumb to form a hollow. Spoon filling into piping bag fitted with 7mm fluted tube, pipe filling into pastry cases. Serve topped with parsley.

Filling Combine celeriac and cream in small pan, simmer, uncovered, about 15 minutes or until celeriac is tender and cream thickened. Blend or process celeriac mixture and cheese until smooth; cover, refrigerate 2 hours. Beat sour cream in small bowl with electric mixer until thick, gently fold in celeriac mixture in 2 batches.

Sift flour into bowl, rub in butter (or process flour and butter until mixture resembles breadcrumbs). Add seeds, egg yolk and enough water to make ingredients cling together (or process until ingredients just come together). Press dough into a ball, knead gently on lightly floured surface until smooth. Wrap in plastic, refrigerate 30 minutes.

Roll pastry between sheets of baking paper until 3mm thick. Cut pastry into 30 x 7cm squares, place into 6cm square tartlet tins, prick all over with fork, place tartlet tins on oven trays, refrigerate 30 minutes.

Bake in moderately hot oven about 15 minutes or until browned; cool. Spoon filling into pastry cases, top with barbecued pork, brush with warmed plum sauce, sprinkle with shallots.

Filling Melt butter in pan, add onion, garlic and ginger, cook, stirring, until onions are very soft. Stir in blended cornflour and water, sauces and sherry. Stir over heat until mixture boils and thickens; cool.

MAKES 30

Pastry cases can be made a week ahead.

Storage Airtight container
Freeze Uncooked pastry suitable
Microwave Filling suitable

SPICY PRAWN AND TOMATO SALSA TARTLETS

Cut out tartlets in batches, re-rolling pastry as necessary.

1½ cups (225g) plain flour
¾ teaspoon ground turmeric
125g cold butter, chopped
1 egg yolk
3 teaspoons iced water, approximately

SPICY PRAWNS
40 medium uncooked prawns
40g butter
2 cloves garlic, crushed
2 tablespoons mild sweet chilli sauce

LIME CREAM
½ cup (125ml) mayonnaise
¼ cup (60ml) sour cream
1 teaspoon grated lime rind
1 tablespoon lime juice

TOMATO SALSA
2 small (200g) tomatoes, peeled, seeded, finely chopped
½ small (50g) Spanish onion, finely chopped
1 tablespoon chopped fresh coriander
1 teaspoon lime juice

Sift flour and turmeric into bowl, rub in butter (or process flour, turmeric and butter until mixture resembles bread-crumbs). Add egg yolk and enough water to make ingredients cling together (or process until ingredients just come together). Press dough into a ball, knead gently on lightly floured surface until smooth. Wrap in plastic, refrigerate for 30 minutes.

Roll pastry between sheets of baking paper until 3mm thick. Place 20 x 11cm boat-shaped tartlet tins face down on pastry, allowing 1cm between tins. Cut around tins, leaving a 5mm border.

Gently press pastry into tins, trim edges; prick all over with fork, place tins on oven trays, refrigerate 30 minutes.

Bake pastry cases in moderately hot oven about 15 minutes or until browned; cool. Spoon lime cream into pastry cases, top with 2 spicy prawns and a teaspoon of tomato salsa.

Spicy Prawns Shell prawns, leaving tails intact. Melt butter in pan, add garlic and sauce, cook, stirring, 1 minute. Add prawns, cook, stirring, until prawns are cooked through, drain on absorbent paper; cool.

Lime Cream Combine all ingredients in bowl, mix well.

Tomato Salsa Combine all ingredients in bowl; mix well.

MAKES 20

Pastry cases can be made a week ahead.

Storage Airtight container
Freeze Uncooked pastry suitable
Microwave Spicy prawns suitable

Top left Blue cheese and celeriac bites
Left Barbecued pork with plum glaze tartlets
Above Spicy prawn and tomato salsa tartlets

CURRIED BEEF SACHETS WITH TOMATO SAUCE

1¹/₂ cups (225g) plain flour
¹/₂ teaspoon ground turmeric
1 tablespoon vegetable oil
¹/₃ cup (80ml) warm water, approximately
1 egg, lightly beaten
1 teaspoon poppy seeds

FILLING
1 tablespoon vegetable oil
1 medium (150g) onion, finely chopped
1 clove garlic, crushed
¹/₂ teaspoon hot curry powder
200g minced beef
¹/₄ cup (40g) pine nuts
¹/₂ cup (60g) frozen peas, thawed
1 tablespoon soy sauce
1 teaspoon beef stock powder
2 tablespoons tomato paste

TOMATO SAUCE
1 tablespoon olive oil
1 small (80g) onion, finely chopped
425g can tomato puree
1 cup (250ml) beef stock
¹/₂ teaspoon sugar

Sift flour and turmeric into bowl, add oil and enough water to make ingredients cling together. Knead dough gently on lightly floured surface until smooth, wrap in plastic, refrigerate 30 minutes.

Divide pastry in half, roll each half on floured surface to a 20cm x 30cm rectangle, cut into 10cm squares. Repeat with remaining pastry. Place a tablespoon of filling in centre of each square, lightly brush edges with egg. Bring up corners to centre, pinch edges to seal.

Place sachets on greased oven tray, brush with egg, sprinkle 2 opposite sides with poppy seeds. Bake in moderately hot oven about 25 minutes or until browned. Serve with tomato sauce.

Filling Heat oil in pan, add onion, garlic and curry powder, cook, stirring, until onion is soft. Add mince, cook, stirring, until mince is changed in colour. Stir in remaining ingredients; mix well.

Tomato Sauce Heat oil in pan, add onion, cook, stirring, until soft. Add puree, stock and sugar, simmer, uncovered, about 20 minutes or until reduced by half.

MAKES 12

Filling and sauce can be made a day ahead.

Storage Covered, separately, in refrigerator
Freeze Uncooked sachets suitable
Microwave Not suitable

SPICY CAJUN-STYLE PIZZAS

1¹/₂ quantities basic shortcrust pastry; recipe page 112
1 small (150g) red pepper
1 small (150g) green pepper
1 small (150g) yellow pepper
120g csabai salami, sliced
1¹/₄ cups (125g) grated mozzarella cheese

TOMATO SAUCE
1 tablespoon olive oil
1 small (80g) onion, chopped
2 cloves garlic, crushed
¹/₄ teaspoon sambal oelek
425g can tomatoes
1 tablespoon tomato paste
1 tablespoon paprika
1 teaspoon chopped fresh thyme
1 teaspoon sugar
pinch cayenne pepper

Make pastry according to directions on page 112. Divide pastry into 6 portions. Roll each portion between sheets of baking paper until large enough to cut into a 16cm round. Place pastry rounds onto greased oven trays, prick well with fork, refrigerate 30 minutes. Bake in moderately hot oven about 20 minutes or until browned; cool.

Quarter peppers, remove seeds and membranes. Grill peppers, skin side up, until skin blisters and blackens. Peel away skin, cut peppers into strips.

Spread pastry rounds with tomato sauce, top with salami. Arrange peppers in a lattice pattern; sprinkle with cheese. Bake in moderate oven about 20 minutes or until cheese is melted.

Tomato Sauce Heat oil in pan, add onion, garlic and sambal oelek, cook, stirring, until onion is soft. Add undrained crushed tomatoes and remaining ingredients, simmer, uncovered, about 15 minutes or until thick.

MAKES 6

Pastry bases can be made 5 days ahead.

Storage Airtight container
Freeze Uncooked pastry suitable
Microwave Not suitable

EGGPLANT, YOGURT AND MINT TRIANGLES

3 sheets ready-rolled puff pastry
1 egg, lightly beaten
2 teaspoons milk
1 tablespoon sesame seeds

FILLING
1 medium (300g) eggplant, chopped
coarse cooking salt
2 tablespoons olive oil
2 cloves garlic, crushed
1 teaspoon ground cumin
1 small (80g) onion, chopped
2 tablespoons pine nuts
1/2 cup (125ml) plain yogurt
2 tablespoons chopped fresh mint
1/2 cup (35g) stale breadcrumbs

Cut each sheet of pastry into 9 x 7.5cm squares. Place a rounded teaspoon of filling in centre of each pastry square. Lightly brush edges with combined egg and milk, fold in half to form triangles, press edges together to seal.

Place triangles on greased oven trays, brush with combined egg and milk, sprinkle with seeds. Bake triangles in very hot oven about 12 minutes or until lightly browned and heated through.

Filling Place eggplant on wire rack (or in colander) sprinkle with salt, stand 30 minutes. Rinse eggplant under cold water, drain on absorbent paper. Heat oil in pan, add eggplant, garlic, cumin, onion and nuts, cook, stirring, until eggplant is soft and nuts are lightly browned; cool. Combine eggplant mixture, yogurt, mint and breadcrumbs in bowl; mix well.

MAKES 27

Triangles can be made a day ahead.

Storage Covered, in refrigerator
Freeze Cooked triangles suitable
Microwave Not suitable

LEMONY SMOKED OYSTER POUCHES

4 x 105g cans smoked oysters, drained, chopped
2/3 cup (100g) pine nuts, toasted
1 cup (70g) stale breadcrumbs
1 tablespoon chopped fresh parsley
1 1/2 teaspoons grated lemon rind
1/3 cup (80ml) lemon juice
9 sheets fillo pastry
150g butter, melted

Combine oysters, nuts, breadcrumbs, parsley, rind and juice in bowl. Layer 3 sheets of pastry together, brushing each with butter. Cut layered sheets into 12 squares. Place a rounded teaspoon of oyster mixture in centre of each square, bring edges together in centre, press firmly to seal. Repeat with remaining pastry, butter and filling. Place pouches onto greased oven trays. Bake in moderately hot oven about 20 minutes or until lightly browned.

MAKES 36

Recipe can be prepared a day ahead.

Storage Covered, in refrigerator
Freeze Uncooked pouches suitable
Microwave Not suitable

Left, from left Curried beef sachets with tomato sauce; Spicy Cajun-style pizzas
Below, from top Lemony smoked oyster pouches; Eggplant, yogurt and mint triangles

RATATOUILLE PALMIERS

2 sheets ready-rolled puff pastry
1 egg, lightly beaten
¹/₂ cup (40g) grated
    parmesan cheese

FILLING
1 tablespoon olive oil
3 green shallots, chopped
1 medium (60g) finger eggplant,
    finely chopped
1 medium (120g) zucchini,
    finely chopped
¹/₂ small (75g) yellow pepper,
    finely chopped
1 small (100g) tomato,
    finely chopped
1 teaspoon chopped fresh thyme
2 tablespoons tomato paste
¹/₃ cup (80ml) water

Spread half the filling over 1 sheet of pastry; repeat with remaining filling and pastry. Fold in sides of each pastry sheet so they meet in the centre, flatten lightly, brush with egg, fold in half again, press lightly, cover, refrigerate 30 minutes.

    Cut pastry into 1cm slices, place cut side up on greased oven trays, sprinkle with cheese. Bake in hot oven about 20 minutes or until browned.

Filling Heat oil in pan, add shallots, cook, stirring, until soft. Add remaining ingredients, simmer, uncovered, about 15 minutes, stirring occasionally, or until thickened cool. Cover, refrigerate 2 hours.

MAKES ABOUT 40

Palmiers can be made a day ahead.

Storage Airtight container
Freeze Uncooked palmiers suitable
Microwave Not suitable

Right, from top Chicken liver pate and herb puffs; Ratatouille Palmiers
Far right Prosciutto, onion and pepper bonbons

CHICKEN LIVER PATE AND HERB PUFFS

1/2 cup (125ml) water
40g butter, chopped
1/2 cup (75g) plain flour
2 eggs, lightly beaten
2 tablespoons chopped fresh parsley
2 tablespoons redcurrant jelly

CHICKEN LIVER PATE
15g butter
2 teaspoons vegetable oil
1/2 small (40g) onion,
    finely chopped
1 clove garlic, crushed
250g chicken livers
1 teaspoon chopped fresh thyme
2 tablespoons beef stock
2 tablespoons brandy
100g soft butter, extra

Combine water and butter in pan, bring to boil, stirring, until butter is melted. Add sifted flour all at once, stir vigorously over heat until mixture leaves side of pan and forms a smooth ball.

Transfer mixture to small bowl of electric mixer (or into processor). Add eggs 1 at a time, beat on low speed until smooth after each addition; mixture should be glossy. Stir in parsley.

Spoon mixture into piping bag fitted with 1.5cm plain tube. Pipe mixture into 2cm rounds about 2cm apart on greased oven trays. Bake in hot oven 10 minutes, reduce heat to moderately hot, bake further 15 minutes or until browned and crisp. Cool on wire rack. Cut puffs in half, fill with some of the chicken liver pate and redcurrant jelly.

Chicken Liver Pate Heat butter and oil in pan, add onion and garlic, cook, stirring until onion is soft. Using a slotted spoon, transfer onion mixture to processor.

Add livers to same pan, cook over high heat until livers are lightly browned and tender. Transfer livers to processor. Add thyme, stock and brandy to same pan, simmer until reduced by half, pour over onion and liver mixture, process mixture until smooth.

With motor operating, add extra butter, a small piece at a time, process until smooth. Push pate through sieve into bowl, cover, refrigerate several hours or until firm. Remove from refrigerator 30 minutes before using.

MAKES 30

Recipe can be made a day ahead.

Storage Pate, covered, in refrigerator
Puffs, in airtight container
Freeze Unfilled puffs suitable
Microwave Not suitable

PROSCIUTTO, ONION AND PEPPER BONBONS

1 tablespoon vegetable oil
15g butter
1 small (80g) onion, sliced
1 clove garlic, crushed
1/2 medium (100g) red pepper
3 sheets fillo pastry
60g butter, melted, extra
2 tablespoons, walnuts,
    toasted, chopped
5 slices (50g) prosciutto, chopped
1 tablespoon chopped fresh basil

Heat oil and butter in pan, add onion and garlic, cook, stirring, until onion is very soft and lightly browned; drain on absorbent paper; cool.

Cut pepper in half, remove seeds and membranes. Grill pepper, skin side up, until skin blisters and blackens. Peel away skin, slice pepper into 16 long strips.

Layer pastry sheets together, brushing each with extra butter. Cut pastry into quarters, cut each quarter into quarters again. Top each quarter evenly with onion mixture, pepper, nuts, prosciutto and basil, roll up from narrow sides, press down ends with fork to form bonbon shapes. Place bonbons on greased oven tray. Bake in hot oven about 10 minutes or until lightly browned and crisp.

MAKES 16

Bonbons can be made a day ahead.

Storage Covered, in refrigerator
Freeze Uncooked bonbons suitable
Microwave Not suitable

CREAMY MUSHROOM AND DILL PASTRY BASKETS

3 sheets fillo pastry
60g butter, melted
2 slices (20g) prosciutto
fresh dill sprigs

FILLING
50g butter
1 medium (150g) onion,
 finely chopped
1 clove garlic, crushed
250g button mushrooms, sliced
250g flat mushrooms, chopped
1/4 cup (60ml) sour cream
1 tablespoon chopped fresh dill

Cut each pastry sheet in half, then each half into 4 squares. Brush 4 squares with butter, layer together at angles, place into 6 x 11cm pie tins. Repeat with remaining pastry and butter. Bake in moderately hot oven about 10 minutes or until browned.

Place prosciutto on oven tray, bake in hot oven about 10 minutes or until crisp; chop finely. Divide filling between pastry baskets, sprinkle with prosciutto and dill.

Filling Heat butter in pan, add onion and garlic, cook, stirring, until onion is soft. Add mushrooms, cook, stirring, until mushrooms are soft and liquid evaporated. Stir in sour cream and dill.

MAKES 6

Pastry baskets and filling can be prepared a day ahead.

Storage Pastry baskets, in airtight container. Filling, covered, in refrigerator
Freeze Not suitable
Microwave Filling suitable

CORN AND PEA SAMOSAS IN CARAWAY SEED PASTRY

The samosa presser is available from Asian grocery stores.

1 1/2 cups (225g) plain flour
30g ghee
1 tablespoon caraway seeds
1/2 cup (125ml) warm water,
 approximately
vegetable oil for deep-frying

FILLING
20g ghee
1/2 small (40g) onion,
 finely chopped
2 cloves garlic, crushed
2 teaspoons grated fresh ginger
2 teaspoons garam masala
1/2 teaspoon ground cumin
1/2 teaspoon ground coriander
1/4 teaspoon ground turmeric
1/4 teaspoon chilli powder
130g can corn kernels,
 rinsed, drained
2/3 (80g) frozen peas, thawed
1/4 cup (60ml) coconut milk

Sift flour into bowl, rub in ghee, add seeds, gradually stir in enough water to mix to a firm dough. Knead on floured surface until smooth. Cover, refrigerate 30 minutes.

Roll pastry on floured surface until 2mm thick. Cut pastry into 9.5cm rounds. Place a rounded teaspoon of filling in centre of each round, brush edges with water.

Press edges together with thumb and finger to seal (or use a samosa presser).

Repeat with remaining pastry and filling. Deep-fry samosas in hot oil until browned.

Filling Heat ghee in pan, add onion, garlic, ginger and spices, stir over heat until onion is soft. Add corn, peas and coconut milk, bring to boil, remove from heat; cool to room temperature.

MAKES ABOUT 20

Samosas can be made a day ahead.

Storage Covered, in refrigerator
Freeze Uncooked samosas suitable
Microwave Not suitable

KUMARA PASTRIES WITH PUMPKIN DHAL

3 cups (450g) plain flour
150g cold butter, chopped
1 tablespoon cumin seeds
2 eggs yolks
1/3 cup (80ml) iced water, approximately
1 egg, lightly beaten

FILLING
150g kumara
1 small (120g) potato
1 tablespoon vegetable oil
2 cloves garlic, crushed
1 teaspoon ground cumin
1/2 teaspoon ground coriander
2 teaspoons paprika
400g minced beef
1 small beef stock cube
1 small (150g) red pepper, finely chopped
1/2 cup (125ml) water

PUMPKIN DHAL
400g pumpkin, chopped
1 teaspoon curry powder
1/2 teaspoon paprika
310g can chickpeas, rinsed, drained
1/2 cup (125ml) sour cream
1 tablespoon chopped fresh parsley

Sift flour into bowl, rub in butter (or process flour and butter until mixture resembles breadcrumbs). Add seeds, egg yolks and enough water to make ingredients cling together (or process until ingredients just come together).

Press dough into a ball, knead gently on lightly floured surface until smooth. Wrap in plastic, refrigerate 30 minutes.

Divide pastry into 6 portions. Roll each portion between sheets of baking paper to a 19cm circle. Place 1/2 cup (125ml) filling onto each circle, brush edges with water, fold in half, press edges together to seal.

Brush pastries with egg. Cut 2 slits in each pastry, place on greased oven trays. Bake in moderately hot oven about 25 minutes or until browned. Serve hot or cold with pumpkin dhal.

Filling Cut kumara and potato into 5mm cubes. Heat oil in pan, add garlic, spices and mince, stir over heat until mince is browned. Add kumara, potato, crumbled stock cube, pepper and water, simmer, uncovered, until vegetables are tender and liquid is evaporated; cool.

Pumpkin Dhal Boil, steam or microwave pumpkin until tender. Add spices to dry pan, cook, stirring, until fragrant, stir in pumpkin and chickpeas; cool. Blend or process mixture until smooth, stir in sour cream and parsley.

MAKES 6

Pastries can be prepared a day ahead. Dhal can be made 3 days ahead.

Storage Covered, separately, in refrigerator
Freeze Uncooked pastries suitable
Microwave Pumpkin suitable

Left, from top Creamy mushroom and dill pastry baskets; Corn and pea samosas in caraway seed pastry
Below Kumara pastries with pumpkin dhal

Seafood

Enjoy the bounty of the sea in delicious and interesting ways. Among the recipes in this section we have koulibiac, a tasty pie from Russia, an onion and anchovy tart from France, a special-occasion lobster in puff pastry treat and a dish combining fresh salmon, spicy tomato and fillo pastry.

PISSALADIERE

1 1/2 cups (225g) plain flour
3/4 cup (105g) self-raising flour
50g cold butter, chopped
1 egg yolk
1 egg, lightly beaten
1/3 cup (80ml) iced water, approximately
2 tablespoons olive oil
30g butter, extra
5 large (1kg) onions, sliced
2 cloves garlic, crushed
2 x 56g cans anchovy fillets, drained
1/2 cup (60g) black olives

TOMATO SAUCE
1 tablespoon olive oil
6 green shallots, chopped
425 can tomatoes

Grease 21cm x 28.5cm rectangular loose-base flan tin. Sift flours into bowl, rub in butter (or process flours and butter until mixture resembles breadcrumbs). Add egg yolk, egg and enough water to make ingredients cling together (or process until ingredients just come together). Press dough into a ball, knead gently on lightly floured surface until smooth. Wrap in plastic, refrigerate dough 30 minutes.

Roll pastry between sheets of baking paper until large enough to line prepared tin. Lift pastry into tin, ease into sides, trim edges. Lightly prick base with fork, refrigerate 30 minutes.

Cover pastry with baking paper, fill with dried beans or rice, place on oven tray. Bake in moderately hot oven 10 minutes. Remove paper and beans carefully from pastry case, bake further 10 minutes or until lightly browned; cool.

Heat oil and extra butter in pan, add onions and garlic, cook, covered, over low heat, stirring occasionally, about 30 minutes, or until onions are very soft but not browned; drain onions on absorbent paper.

Cut each anchovy fillet into 3 long strips. Spread base of pastry case with tomato sauce, top with onion mixture. Place olives and anchovies in lattice pattern. Bake in moderately hot oven about 15 minutes or until heated through.

Tomato Sauce Heat oil in pan, add shallots, cook, stirring, until soft. Add undrained crushed tomatoes, simmer, uncovered, stirring occasionally, about 10 minutes or until thick.

SERVES 6
Recipe can be made 3 hours ahead.

Storage Covered, in refrigerator
Freeze Uncooked pastry suitable
Microwave Not suitable

KOULIBIAC

1 cup (250ml) water
1 cup (250ml) dry white wine
1 small (80g) onion, chopped
1 stick celery, chopped
1 small (70g) carrot, chopped
8 black peppercorns
500g ocean trout fillets
80g butter
2 small (160g) onions,
  chopped, extra
250g button mushrooms, sliced
1 cup (200g) long-grain rice
1 cup (250ml) chicken stock
2 tablespoons chopped fresh parsley
500g packet ready-rolled, puff
  pastry roll, thawed
3 hard-boiled eggs, sliced
1 egg yolk

DILL SAUCE
300ml sour cream
2 tablespoons chopped fresh dill
2 teaspoons lemon juice
$1/2$ teaspoon sugar

Combine water, wine, onion, celery, carrot and peppercorns in large pan, bring to boil, reduce heat, add trout. Simmer, covered, about 10 minutes or until cooked through. Remove trout from pan, drain on absorbent paper; cool. Discard skin and bones; flake trout. Strain poaching liquid; reserve 1 cup (250ml) liquid, discard pulp.

Heat half the butter in pan, add half the extra onions, cook, stirring, until soft. Add mushrooms, cook, stirring, until mushrooms are just soft; cool.

Heat remaining butter in pan, add remaining extra onions, cook, stirring, until onions are soft.

Add rice, stir until rice is coated in butter. Add stock and reserved poaching liquid, simmer, covered, over very low heat about 15 minutes or until rice is tender and all liquid absorbed. Stir in parsley; cool.

Unroll pastry, cut into 35cm length, place on greased oven tray. Spread rice mixture over pastry, leaving 5cm border.

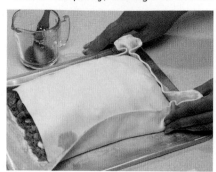

Top with hard-boiled eggs, trout and mushroom mixture. Cut 5cm strip from long edge of remaining pastry, cut strip into fish shapes. Place remaining pastry on top of pie. Brush edges with egg yolk, fold pastry up over sides of pie; pinch edges to seal.

Decorate pie with fish shapes; brush with egg yolk. Bake in hot oven about 30 minutes or until browned and heated through. Serve with dill sauce.

Dill Sauce Combine all ingredients in small bowl; mix well.

SERVES 6 TO 8

Recipe can be prepared a day ahead.

Storage Covered, separately, in refrigerator
Freeze Uncooked pie suitable
Microwave Fish, mushrooms and rice suitable

WHOLEMEAL SMOKED COD AND TOMATO PIES

1 quantity basic wholemeal pastry; recipe page 112
1 egg yolk
2 teaspoons milk
400g smoked cod fillets
1 cup (250ml) water
1 cup (250ml) milk, extra
2 bay leaves
1 teaspoon black peppercorns

TOMATO FILLING
2 tablespoons olive oil
1 medium (350g) leek, sliced
2 cloves garlic, crushed
3 large (750g) tomatoes, peeled, seeded, chopped
2 tablespoons tomato paste
2 teaspoons chopped fresh oregano
1 strip lemon rind
1 tablespoon chopped fresh parsley

Grease 4 x 12cm oval pie tins. Make pastry according to directions on page 112. Divide pastry into 4 portions. Roll each portion between sheets of baking paper until large enough to line prepared tins. Lift pastry into tins, ease pastry into sides, trim edges.

Cut fish shapes from pastry scraps. Brush edges of pastry cases with combined egg yolk and milk, place fish shapes overlapping around edges. Brush shapes with egg yolk mixture. Lightly prick bases with fork, refrigerate 30 minutes.

Cover pastry with baking paper, fill with dried beans or rice, place on oven tray. Bake in moderately hot oven 10 minutes. Remove paper and beans carefully from pastry cases, bake further 10 minutes or until lightly browned; cool.

Combine cod, water, extra milk, bay leaves and peppercorns in pan, simmer, uncovered, about 10 minutes or until cod is tender. Drain cod, discard milk mixture. Remove skin from cod, flake cod into large pieces. Just before serving, stir cod into tomato filling; spoon mixture into pastry cases.

Tomato Filling Heat oil in pan, add leek and garlic, cook, stirring, until leek is soft. Add tomatoes, paste, oregano and rind, cook, stirring, 5 minutes; remove and discard rind. Stir in parsley.

MAKES 4

Pastry cases, cod and tomato filling can be prepared a day ahead.

Storage Pastry cases, in airtight container. Cod and tomato filling, covered, separately, in refrigerator
Freeze Not suitable
Microwave Cod and tomato filling suitable

Left Koulibiac
Above Wholemeal smoked cod and tomato pies

SARDINE AND OLIVE QUICHE

1³/₄ cups (255g) plain flour
150g cold butter, chopped
1 egg yolk
2 tablespoons iced water,
    approximately
2 teaspoons olive oil
15g butter, extra
1 medium (150g) onion, sliced
1 clove garlic, crushed
105g can sardines, drained, chopped
2 medium (260g) tomatoes, peeled,
    seeded, quartered
2 tablespoons chopped seedless
    black olives
2 tablespoons chopped drained
    sun-dried tomatoes
2 tablespoons grated
    parmesan cheese

FILLING
2 eggs, lightly beaten
¹/₂ cup (125ml) creme fraiche
1 tablespoon cream
2 tablespoons grated
    parmesan cheese
1 clove garlic, crushed
1 tablespoon chopped fresh parsley
1 tablespoon chopped fresh basil

Grease 24cm round loose-base flan tin.
Sift flour into bowl; rub in butter (or
process flour and butter until mixture
resembles breadcrumbs). Add egg yolk
and enough water to make ingredients
cling together (or process until
ingredients just come together). Press
dough into a ball, knead gently on lightly
floured surface until smooth. Wrap in
plastic, refrigerate 30 minutes.

Roll pastry between sheets of baking
paper until large enough to line prepared
tin. Lift pastry into tin, ease into side,
trim edge, refrigerate 30 minutes.

Cover pastry with baking paper, fill
with dried beans or rice, place on oven
tray. Bake in moderately hot oven
10 minutes. Remove paper and beans
carefully from pastry case, bake further
10 minutes or until lightly browned; cool.

Heat oil and extra butter in pan, add
onion and garlic, cook, stirring, until
onion is soft and browned, drain on
absorbent paper, cool. Place sardines and
tomatoes in pastry case, sprinkle with
onion mixture, olives and sun-dried
tomatoes. Pour over filling, sprinkle with
cheese. Bake in moderately hot oven
about 35 minutes or until filling is set.

Filling Combine all ingredients in bowl;
mix well.

SERVES 6

Recipe can be made a day ahead.

Storage Covered, in refrigerator
Freeze Uncooked pastry suitable
Microwave Not suitable

LOBSTER AND SEAFOOD PIE

2 (400g) uncooked lobster tails
400g firm white fish fillets
50g butter
2 tablespoons olive oil
200g scallops
2 medium (300g) onions, sliced
4 cloves garlic, crushed
500g packet ready-rolled puff
    pastry roll, thawed
1 egg, lightly beaten

WINE CREAM SAUCE
90g butter
1/2 cup (75g) plain flour
2/3 cup (160ml) milk
1/2 cup (125ml) cream
1 cup (250ml) fish stock
2/3 cup (160ml) dry white wine
1/2 cup (40g) grated
    parmesan cheese
1 tablespoon chopped fresh dill
1 tablespoon chopped fresh parsley

Remove lobster meat from tails, cut into 1cm thick medallions. Cut fish into 2cm pieces. Heat butter and oil in pan, cook lobster, fish and scallops separately in batches, stirring, until just tender, drain on absorbent paper. Add onions and garlic to same pan, cook, stirring, until onions are soft; drain on absorbent paper.

Combine seafood, onion mixture and wine cream sauce in bowl, mix well; cool. Pour mixture into 20cm x 26cm (1.5 litre/6 cup capacity) ovenproof dish. Cut a length of pastry from the pastry roll large enough to extend 4cm over sides of dish. Fold overhanging pastry onto the edges of the dish to form a rim, press pastry to seal.

Cut 3 large starfish shapes from some of the remaining pastry, place on pie, using a little beaten egg. Brush pie with egg. Bake in hot oven about 35 minutes or until pastry is browned.

Wine Cream Sauce Melt butter in pan, stir in flour, stir over heat until bubbling. Remove from heat, gradually stir in milk, cream, stock and wine, stir over heat until mixture boils and thickens. Remove from heat, stir in cheese and herbs.

SERVES 6

Recipe can be prepared 3 hours ahead.

Storage Covered, in refrigerator
Freeze Not suitable
Microwave Not suitable

From left Lobster and seafood pie; Tomato, sardine and olive quiche

SMOKED SALMON AND ASPARAGUS QUICHE

**1 quantity basic shortcrust pastry;
  recipe page 112**
1 bunch (250g) fresh asparagus
5 eggs
1/2 cup (125ml) milk
2 teaspoons chopped fresh dill
150g smoked salmon
1 tablespoon olive oil
**1 medium (150g) onion,
  finely chopped**

Make pastry according to directions on page 112. Roll pastry between sheets of baking paper until large enough to line 24cm round loose-base flan tin. Lift pastry into tin, ease into side, trim edge.

Lightly prick base with fork, refrigerate 30 minutes.

Cover pastry with baking paper, fill with dried beans or rice, place on oven tray. Bake in moderately hot oven 10 minutes. Remove paper and beans carefully from pastry case, bake further 10 minutes or until lightly browned; cool.

Cut asparagus 10cm from the tips, reserve tips. Chop remaining asparagus into 2cm pieces. Blend or process eggs, milk and dill until combined. Cut salmon into thin strips.

Heat oil in pan, add chopped asparagus and onion, cook, stirring, until onion is soft, remove from heat, stir in salmon. Spread mixture into pastry case; pour in egg mixture. Bake in moderate oven about 1 hour or until lightly browned.

Boil, steam or microwave reserved asparagus tips until just tender; drain. Serve quiche topped with asparagus tips.

SERVES 6

Recipe can be made a day ahead.

Storage Covered, in refrigerator
Freeze Suitable
Microwave Asparagus tips suitable

CUCUMBER SAMBAL

2 small (240g) green cucumbers, seeded, chopped
3 green shallots, chopped
1/2 cup (125ml) sour cream
2 tablespoons chopped fresh mint

Heat butter in pan, add salmon, cook quickly over high heat on both sides until browned but not cooked through; drain salmon on absorbent paper.

Layer 2 pastry sheets together, brushing each with extra butter, fold pastry in half. Place salmon in centre of pastry, top with a quarter of tomato chilli sauce, fold pastry to form a parcel and enclose salmon, brush parcel with more extra butter. Repeat with remaining pastry, extra butter, salmon and tomato chilli sauce. Place parcels on greased oven tray, bake in hot oven about 15 minutes or until browned. Serve with cucumber sambal.

Tomato Chilli Sauce Heat oil in pan, add onion and garlic, cook, stirring, until onion is soft. Stir in undrained crushed tomatoes, wine, paste and sambal oelek. Simmer, uncovered, about 15 minutes or until thick, stir in basil; cool.

Cucumber Sambal Combine all ingredients in bowl; mix well.

MAKES 4

Recipe can be prepared 3 hours ahead.

Storage Covered, in refrigerator
Freeze Not suitable
Microwave Not suitable

Left Smoked salmon and asparagus quiche
Below Fresh salmon and spicy tomato parcels

FRESH SALMON AND SPICY TOMATO PARCELS

30g butter
4 (800g) fresh salmon fillets, skinned
8 sheets fillo pastry
60g butter, melted, extra

TOMATO CHILLI SAUCE

1 tablespoon olive oil
1 medium (150g) onion, chopped
1 clove garlic, crushed
425g can tomatoes
2 tablespoons dry red wine
1 tablespoon tomato paste
1/2 teaspoon sambal oelek
1 tablespoon chopped fresh basil

Poultry

There are so many ideas for deliciously different entrees, light lunches and main courses in this section. Tantalising treats include olive and pimiento chicken in fillo, duck and parsnip tarts and creamed turkey under a pastry lattice. Chicken is always a popular choice because it's delicious, low in fat, high in protein and suitable for absolutely every occasion.

OLIVE AND PIMIENTO CHICKEN IN FILLO

20 large English spinach leaves
1 canned pimiento, drained
1 small (90g) zucchini
4 chicken thigh fillets
4 slices mozzarella cheese
2 tablespoons olive paste
12 sheets fillo pastry
80g butter, melted

MUSTARD SAUCE
1/3 cup (80ml) thickened cream
1/4 cup (60ml) sour cream
1 teaspoon French mustard
2 teaspoons seeded mustard
2 teaspoons chopped fresh chives

Add spinach to pan of boiling water; drain immediately, rinse under cold water, drain well. Cut pimiento and zucchini into strips. Place chicken, smooth side down, on bench, pound gently between layers of plastic wrap to flatten slightly.

Divide pimiento, zucchini and cheese crossways over fillets, fold fillets in half to enclose filling. Spread 2 teaspoons of the olive paste over fillets, roll each fillet in 5 overlapped spinach leaves.

Layer 3 pastry sheets together, brushing each with butter. Place 1 prepared fillet at narrow end of pastry, roll once, fold in sides; continue rolling to form a parcel, leaving open side facing up. Fold 1cm width of pastry edge back, to give a pleated effect. Brush with more butter, place on greased oven tray. Repeat with remaining pastry, butter and prepared fillets.

Bake in moderate oven about 10 minutes or until lightly browned, cover loosely with foil, bake further 35 minutes or until pastry is browned. Serve with mustard sauce.

Mustard Sauce Combine all ingredients in bowl; mix well.

SERVES 4

Recipe can be prepared a day ahead.

Storage Covered, in refrigerator
Freeze Not suitable
Microwave Not suitable

CHICKEN AND LEEK PIE

2 cups (300g) plain flour
1 cup (170g) cornmeal
125g packet cream cheese, chopped
60g cold butter, chopped
2 egg yolks
1/3 cup (80ml) iced water,
    approximately
1/3 cup (80ml) vegetable oil
800g chicken thigh fillets, sliced
4 medium (800g) potatoes,
    peeled, sliced
60g butter, extra
500g button mushrooms, sliced
3 medium (1kg) leeks, sliced
4 bacon rashers, chopped
2 cloves garlic, crushed
2 tablespoons French mustard
1 tablespoon chopped fresh thyme
1/2 teaspoon paprika

Grease 30cm pie dish (2.5 litre/10 cup capacity). Sift flour into bowl, stir in cornmeal. Rub in cheese and butter (or process flour, cornmeal, cheese and butter until mixture resembles breadcrumbs). Add egg yolks and enough water to make ingredients cling together (or process until ingredients just come together). Press dough into a ball, knead gently on floured surface until smooth. Wrap in plastic, refrigerate 30 minutes.

Reserve one-third of the pastry for topping. Wrap in plastic; freeze. Roll remaining pastry between sheets of baking paper until large enough to line prepared dish. Lift pastry into dish, ease into side, trim edge. Lightly prick base with fork, refrigerate 30 minutes.

Cover pastry with baking paper, fill with dried beans or rice, place on oven tray. Bake in moderately hot oven 15 minutes. Remove paper and beans carefully from pastry case, bake further 15 minutes or until lightly browned; cool.

Heat 1 tablespoon of the oil in pan, add chicken in batches, cook, stirring, until browned; drain on absorbent paper. Heat remaining oil in same pan, add potatoes in batches, cook until browned on both sides; drain on absorbent paper.

Heat extra butter in pan, add mushrooms, leeks, bacon and garlic, cook, stirring, until leeks are soft. Stir in chicken, mustard and thyme. Cool 10 minutes.

Place half the potato over pastry base, top with chicken mixture, then remaining potato; press gently. Grate reserved frozen pastry over filling, sprinkle with paprika. Bake in moderate oven about 40 minutes or until pie is browned.

SERVES 6

Recipe can be made a day ahead.

Storage Covered, in refrigerator
Freeze Suitable
Microwave Not suitable

SMOKED CHICKEN AND MUSHROOM GOUGERES

80g butter
1 cup (250ml) water
1 cup (150g) plain flour
4 eggs
¹/₄ cup (30g) grated gruyere cheese
paprika

FILLING

2 skinless smoked single chicken
    breast fillets
50g butter
1 clove garlic, crushed
100g button mushrooms, sliced
4 green shallots, chopped
1 teaspoon seeded mustard
2 tablespoons plain flour
1 cup (250ml) milk
1 teaspoon chicken stock powder
¹/₂ cup (125ml) water
¹/₄ cup (30g) grated gruyere cheese
1 tablespoon chopped fresh parsley

Grease 4 shallow ovenproof dishes
(1 cup/250ml capacity). Combine butter
and water in pan, bring to boil, stirring,
until butter is melted. Add sifted flour all
at once, stir vigorously over heat until
mixture leaves side of pan and forms a
smooth ball.

Transfer mixture to small bowl of
electric mixer (or into processor). And
eggs 1 at a time, beat on low speed until
smooth after each addition, stir in cheese.

Spoon pastry around the edge of each
dish, leaving a hollow in the centre. Bake
in hot oven about 45 minutes or until
pastry is browned and puffed. Remove
from oven, spoon filling into hollow, bake
further 5 minutes or until filling is hot.
Serve sprinkled with paprika.

Filling Thinly slice chicken fillets. Heat
butter in pan, add garlic, mushrooms,
shallots and mustard, cook, stirring, until
mushrooms are soft. Stir in flour, stir over
heat until mixture is combined. Remove
from heat, gradually stir in combined
milk, stock powder and water. Stir over
heat until mixture boils and thickens, stir
in chicken, cheese and parsley.

SERVES 4

Filling can be made a day ahead.

Storage Covered, in refrigerator
Freeze Not suitable
Microwave Not suitable

CREAMY CHICKEN PIE

5 (850g) single chicken
    breast fillets
60g butter
4 bacon rashers, chopped
6 green shallots, chopped
2 cloves garlic, crushed
¹/₃ cup (50g) plain flour
1¹/₂ cups (375ml) milk
¹/₃ cup (25g) grated
    parmesan cheese
2 eggs, lightly beaten
10 sheets fillo pastry
80g butter, melted, extra

Cook chicken in large pan of simmering
water for about 15 minutes or until
chicken is just tender; drain. Cut chicken
into chunks.

Meanwhile, lightly grease 25cm pie
dish. Heat butter in pan, add bacon,
shallots and garlic, cook, stirring until
bacon is crisp. Add flour, stir until
combined. Remove from heat, gradually
stir in milk, stir over heat until mixture
boils and thickens; cool. Stir in chicken,
cheese and eggs.

Layer 2 pastry sheets together,
brushing each with some of the extra
butter. Fold layered sheets in half
lengthways, brush with more butter,
place in prepared dish allowing edges to
overhang. Repeat with another 6 pastry
sheets and more extra butter, overlapping
strips clockwise around dish until dish
is covered.

Spoon chicken mixture over pastry,
fold overhanging edges back over filling;
brush pie all over with more extra butter.

Layer remaining 2 pastry sheets
together, brushing each with more extra
butter, fold in half crossways, buttered
sides together. Place pastry on top of pie,
trim edge. Brush top lightly with
remaining extra butter, bake in moderate
oven about 45 minutes or until lightly
browned (cover with foil if pie starts to
overbrown).

SERVES 6 TO 8

Recipe can be prepared a day ahead.

Storage Covered, in refrigerator
Freeze Not suitable
Microwave Not suitable

Left, from left Smoked chicken and mushroom
gougeres; Chicken and leek pie
Right Creamy chicken pie

CHICKEN WITH BASIL AND PINE NUTS

2 sheets ready-rolled puff pastry
1/4 cup (20g) parmesan cheese flakes

FILLING
1 tablespoon olive oil
40g butter
500g chicken breast fillets, thinly sliced
2 green shallots, chopped
1 teaspoon seeded mustard
1 tablespoon plain flour
1¼ cups (310ml) milk
½ teaspoon chicken stock powder
½ cup (80g) pine nuts, toasted
½ cup shredded fresh basil
¼ cup (20g) grated parmesan cheese
¼ cup (35g) drained sliced sun-dried tomatoes

Cut both pastry sheets into 24cm rounds. Cut a 19cm circle from centre of 1 round to give a 2.5cm border. Place 24cm round on greased oven tray, prick well with fork.

Brush edge with water, place border on round; use knife to mark sides of pastry so it "puffs" more during cooking.

Preheat oven to highest setting, place pastry in oven, reduce temperature to

hot, bake about 20 minutes or until browned. Press centre of cooked pastry shell with tea-towel to flatten. Spoon filling into pie case; serve topped with cheese flakes.

Filling Heat oil and half the butter in pan, add chicken in batches, cook, stirring, until tender; drain on absorbent paper. Heat remaining butter in pan, add shallots and mustard, cook, stirring, until shallots are soft. Add flour, cook, stirring, until mixture is dry and grainy.

Remove from heat, gradually stir in milk and stock powder, stir until smooth. Stir over heat until sauce boils and thickens; simmer, uncovered, 1 minute; remove from heat. Add chicken, pine nuts, basil, cheese and tomatoes; stir until combined.

SERVES 4
Filling can be made 3 hours ahead.

Storage Covered, in refrigerator
Freeze Not suitable
Microwave Not suitable

SPICY CHICKEN SATAY TART

1 quantity basic shortcrust pastry; recipe page 112
2 teaspoons mild curry powder
1 teaspoon dried crushed chillies
1 teaspoon ground cumin

FILLING
1 tablespoon vegetable oil
4 green shallots, chopped
2 teaspoons mild curry powder
1 teaspoon ground cumin
1 clove garlic, crushed
200g minced chicken
¼ cup (60ml) crunchy peanut butter
1 tablespoon hoi sin sauce
3 eggs, lightly beaten
¼ cup (15g) stale breadcrumbs
1 tablespoon chopped fresh coriander
¼ cup (60ml) coconut milk

Make pastry according to directions on page 112, adding spices to sifted flour. Roll pastry between sheets of baking paper until large enough to line 24cm round loose-base flan tin. Lift pastry into tin, ease into side, trim edge. Lightly prick base with fork, refrigerate 30 minutes.

Cover pastry with baking paper, fill with dried beans or rice, place on oven tray. Bake in moderately hot oven 10 minutes. Remove paper and beans carefully from pastry case, bake further 10 minutes or until lightly browned; cool.

Spread filling into pastry case, decorate with pastry scraps, if desired. Bake in moderate oven about 25 minutes or until filling is lightly browned; cool.

Filling Heat oil in pan, add shallots, curry powder, cumin, garlic and mince, cook, stirring, until mince is changed in colour; cool slightly. Combine mince and remaining ingredients in bowl; mix well.

SERVES 4 TO 6

Tart can be made a day ahead.

Storage Covered, in refrigerator
Freeze Not suitable
Microwave Not suitable

DUCK AND PARSNIP TARTS

1¹/₂ cups (225g) plain flour
³/₄ cup (105g) self-raising flour
50g cold butter, chopped
2 eggs, lightly beaten
¹/₃ cup (80ml) water, approximately

FILLING
2kg duck
8 sprigs fresh thyme
8 sprigs fresh rosemary
4cm piece (30g) fresh ginger, sliced
40g butter
1 medium (150g) onion,
  finely chopped
125g button mushrooms, sliced
1 tablespoon plain flour
³/₄ cup (180ml) chicken stock
2 tablespoons port

TOPPING
1 clove garlic, peeled
3 small (450g) parsnips, chopped
2 small (240g) potatoes, chopped
300ml cream

Grease 4 x 11cm round pie tins. Sift flours into bowl, rub in butter (or process flours and butter until mixture resembles breadcrumbs). Add 1 of the eggs and enough water to make ingredients cling together (or process until ingredients just come together). Press dough into a ball, knead gently on lightly floured surface until smooth. Wrap in plastic, refrigerate 30 minutes.

Divide pastry into 4 portions. Roll each portion between sheets of baking paper until large enough to line prepared tins. Lift pastry into tins, ease into sides. Using scissors, trim pastry so it extends 1.5cm over edge of tin. Cut 1cm-deep slits into pastry edge every 1cm; brush cut edges with remaining beaten egg. Fold over alternate slits, pressing down lightly to secure. Prick bases with fork. Place tins on oven tray, refrigerate 30 minutes.

Cover pastry with baking paper, fill with dried beans or rice. Bake in moderately hot oven 10 minutes. Remove paper and beans carefully from pastry cases, bake further 15 minutes or until browned; cool.

Divide duck mixture evenly between pastry cases. Place a collar of foil around inner edge of each pastry case. Brush inside of foil with oil. Divide topping mixture evenly between pastry cases,

return to oven tray, bake in moderately hot oven about 20 minutes or until heated through. Grill until lightly browned; remove collars.

Filling Fill duck cavity with the herbs and ginger, secure opening with skewer. Place duck on wire rack in baking dish. Bake uncovered in moderately hot oven about 1¹/₂ hours or until duck is browned and tender; cool.

Remove meat from duck. Shred meat, discard skin and bones. Heat butter in pan, add onion, cook, stirring, until soft. Add mushrooms, cook, stirring, until tender. Add flour, cook, stirring, until combined. Gradually add stock and port, cook, stirring, until mixture boils and thickens. Stir in duck meat, cook, uncovered, further 3 minutes; cool.

Topping Press garlic flat with side of knife. Combine parsnips, potatoes, cream and garlic in pan, cook, covered, stirring occasionally, for 5 minutes. Remove lid, simmer further 5 minutes or until vegetables are tender and cream thickened; discard garlic.

SERVES 4

Pastry and filling can be made a day ahead.

Storage Pastry, in airtight container. Duck, covered, in refrigerator
Freeze Uncooked pastry suitable
Microwave Not suitable

Left, from left Chicken with basil and pine nuts; Spicy chicken satay tart
Above Duck and parsnip tarts

Hearty meat

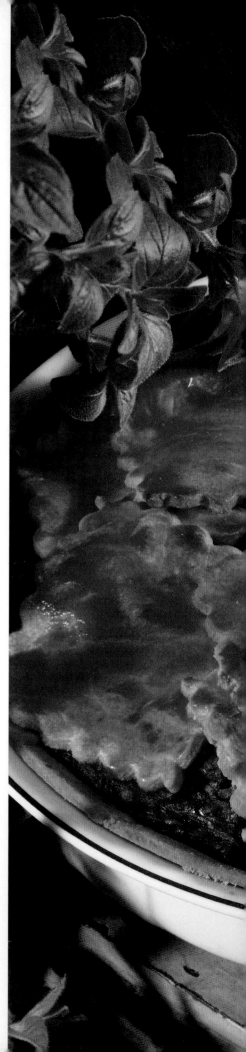

Here are hot 'n' hearty pies and pastries that are just perfect fare for cool winter days. We've included a curried beef pithivier, tasty lamb pie, pork and olive pastries and everybody's favourite, individual Aussie meat pies. Offering a delicious selection of meat cuts, combined with vegetables and herbs, pies and pastries are the perfect choice for a truly satisfying meal for family or friends.

HERBED VEAL AND TOMATO PIE

2¹/2 cups (375g) plain flour
200g cold butter, chopped
3 egg yolks
2 tablespoons iced water, approximately

FILLING
¹/4 cup olive oil
8 baby (200g) onions, halved
1kg diced veal
¹/4 cup (35g) plain flour
2 x 425g cans tomatoes
2 tablespoons tomato paste
¹/4 cup (60ml) dry red wine
2 tablespoons chopped
    fresh oregano
1 tablespoon chopped fresh thyme
1 medium (180g) orange,
    segmented, seeded
250g button mushrooms
2 tablespoons plain flour, extra
2 tablespoons water

Sift flour into bowl, rub in butter (or process flour and butter until mixture resembles breadcrumbs). Add 2 of the egg yolks and enough water to make ingredients cling together (or process until ingredients just come together). Press dough into a ball, knead gently on lightly floured surface until smooth. Wrap in plastic, refrigerate 30 minutes.

Roll three-quarters of the pastry between sheets of baking paper until large enough to line 24cm round pie dish (2 litre/8 cup capacity). Lift pastry into dish, ease into side, trim edge. Cover pastry with baking paper, fill with dried beans or rice; place on oven tray. Bake in moderately hot oven 10 minutes. Remove paper and beans carefully from pastry case, bake further 10 minutes or until pastry is lightly browned; cool.

Roll remaining pastry and scraps until 3mm thick; cut pastry into 13 x 8cm squares. Fill pastry case with filling, top with pastry squares. Brush with a little of the remaining egg yolk, bake in hot oven about 40 minutes or until lightly browned and heated through.

Filling Heat 1 tablespoon of the oil in pan, add onions, cook, stirring, until browned; drain on absorbent paper. Toss veal in flour, shake away excess flour. Heat remaining oil in pan, add veal in batches, cook until browned all over; remove veal from pan.

Add undrained crushed tomatoes, paste and wine to same pan, cook, stirring, until mixture boils and thickens; add herbs. Return veal to pan, simmer, un-covered, 30 minutes, stirring occasionally. Add onions, orange segments and mushrooms, cook further 15 minutes or until veal is tender. Stir in blended extra flour and water, stir over heat until mixture boils and thickens; cool.

SERVES 6

Recipe can be made a day ahead.

Storage Covered, in refrigerator
Freeze Suitable
Microwave Not suitable

RICH LAMB AND POTATO PIE

1 quantity basic shortcrust pastry;
   recipe page 112
1.5kg shoulder of lamb, boned
1 tablespoon olive oil
8 baby (200g) onions, halved
2 cloves garlic, crushed
425g can tomatoes
1/2 cup (125ml) beef stock
3/4 cup (180ml) dry red wine
2 tablespoons chopped
   fresh rosemary
2 large (600g) potatoes, chopped
2 sheets ready-rolled puff pastry
1 egg, lightly beaten

Make pastry according to directions on page 112. Roll pastry between sheets of baking paper until large enough to line deep 25cm pie dish (1.75 litre/7 cup capacity). Lift pastry into dish, ease into side, trim edge. Lightly prick base with fork, cover, refrigerate 30 minutes.

Cover pastry with baking paper, fill with dried beans or rice, place on oven tray. Bake in moderately hot oven 10 minutes. Remove paper and beans carefully from pastry case, bake further 10 minutes or until lightly browned; cool.

Cut lamb into 3cm cubes. Heat oil in pan, add lamb in batches, cook, stirring, until browned; drain on absorbent paper. Add onions and garlic to same pan, cook, stirring, until onions are browned and soft. Return lamb to pan, stir in undrained crushed tomatoes, stock, wine and rosemary. Simmer, covered, 1 1/4 hours, stirring occasionally. Remove lid, simmer further 30 minutes or until lamb is tender.

Boil, steam or microwave potatoes until just tender; drain. Add potatoes to lamb mixture, simmer, uncovered, until sauce is thickened; cool.

Spoon lamb mixture into pastry case, cover with 1 sheet of puff pastry, trim edge. Cut rounds from remaining pastry sheet, brush edge of pastry with egg, place rounds in position, brush pastry with more egg. Bake in hot oven about 30 minutes or until pastry is browned.

SERVES 6

Recipe can be made a day ahead.

Storage Covered, in refrigerator
Freeze Suitable
Microwave Potatoes suitable

Left Rich lamb and potato pie
Right Beef, kumara and oregano pie

BEEF, KUMARA
AND OREGANO PIE

**1 quantity basic shortcrust pastry;
recipe page 112**
1 medium (400g) kumara
800g chuck steak
1/2 cup (75g) plain flour
3 teaspoons paprika
1/4 cup (80ml) vegetable oil
2 medium (300g) onions, sliced
4 bacon rashers, chopped
4 cloves garlic, crushed
1/4 cup chopped fresh oregano
1 tablespoon chopped fresh thyme
1 large (250g) tomato, chopped
1 1/2 cups (375ml) beef stock
1/2 cup (125ml) dry red wine
1/3 cup (80ml) tomato paste
2 tablespoons plain flour, extra
1/4 cup (60ml) water
1 egg yolk
2 teaspoons milk
2 sheets ready-rolled puff pastry

Grease deep 24cm round loose-base flan tin. Make pastry according to directions on page 112. Roll pastry between sheets of baking paper until large enough to line prepared tin. Lift pastry into tin, ease into side, trim edge. Lightly prick base with fork, cover, refrigerate 30 minutes.

Cover pastry with baking paper, fill with dried beans or rice, place on oven tray. Bake in moderately hot oven 20 minutes. Remove paper and beans carefully from pastry case, bake further 10 minutes or until lightly browned; cool.

Cut kumara and steak into 2cm pieces. Place kumara on oven tray, bake in moderate oven about 40 minutes or until tender. Toss steak in combined flour and paprika, shake away excess flour mixture; reserve flour mixture. Heat half the oil in pan, add steak in batches, cook until well browned; remove from pan.

Heat remaining oil in same pan, add onions, bacon, garlic and herbs, cook, stirring, until onions are soft. Return steak to pan, add tomato, stock, wine and paste, simmer, covered, about 1 1/4 hours or until steak is tender. Stir in blended reserved flour mixture, extra flour and

water. Stir over heat until mixture boils and thickens. Stir in kumara; cool.

Spoon filling into pastry case, brush edge of pastry with combined egg yolk and milk. Cover filling with 1 sheet of puff pastry, press edges together firmly, trim edge, brush pie with more egg yolk mixture. Cut remaining puff pastry into 16 x 1.5cm strips. Place strips across pie in a lattice pattern, trim edges, brush with remaining egg yolk mixture. Bake in moderately hot oven about 40 minutes or until browned.

SERVES 6

Recipe can be made a day ahead.

Storage Covered, in refrigerator
Freeze Suitable
Microwave Not suitable

Process pork until finely minced. Heat oil in pan, add onion and garlic, cook, stirring, until onion is soft. Add pork, cook, stirring, until browned. Add wine, juice and blended stock and flour. Stir until mixture boils and thickens, simmer, uncovered, 10 minutes. Remove from heat, stir in olives and oregano; cool.

Divide pastry into 8 portions, roll each portion to 14cm square, trim edges. Divide pork filling between squares, lightly brush edges with water. Fold pastry over filling to form triangles, press edges with fork to seal.

Place triangles on greased oven trays, brush with egg, bake in moderate oven about 30 minutes or until browned. Serve with tomato sauce.

Cornmeal Pastry Process flour and cornmeal briefly to mix. Add butter, process until mixture resembles bread-crumbs. Add enough water to make ingredients cling together and form a firm dough. Knead dough gently on lightly floured surface until smooth; cover, refrigerate 30 minutes.

Tomato Sauce Heat oil in pan, add onion and garlic, cook, stirring, until onion is soft. Add undrained crushed tomatoes, paste, stock and oregano. Simmer, un-covered, about 15 minutes or until thick.

MAKES 8

Recipe can be made a day ahead.

Storage Covered, separately, in refrigerator
Freeze Cooked pastries and tomato sauce suitable
Microwave Not suitable

PORK AND OLIVE PASTRIES

500g pork fillets, chopped
2 tablespoons olive oil
1 medium (150g) onion, chopped
4 cloves garlic, crushed
1/4 cup (60ml) dry red wine
1 tablespoon lemon juice
1 cup (250ml) chicken stock
1 1/2 tablespoons plain flour
10 seedless black olives, sliced
1/4 cup chopped fresh oregano
1 egg, lightly beaten

CORNMEAL PASTRY
2 cups (300g) plain flour
1/4 cup (40g) cornmeal
125g cold butter, chopped
1/3 cup (80ml) iced water, approximately

TOMATO SAUCE
1 tablespoon olive oil
1 medium (150g) onion, chopped
2 cloves garlic, crushed
425g can tomatoes
2 tablespoons tomato paste
1/2 cup (125ml) chicken stock
1 tablespoon chopped fresh oregano

CABBAGE, BACON AND ONION STRUDEL

40g butter
2 medium (300g) onions, sliced
4 bacon rashers, chopped
1/4 medium (375g) cabbage, shredded
2 tablespoons chopped fresh thyme
1 tablespoon chopped fresh parsley
8 sheets fillo pastry
50g butter, melted, extra
2 hard-boiled eggs, sliced
1/2 teaspoon poppy seeds

APPLE SAUCE
2 medium (300g) apples, peeled, cored, chopped
1/3 cup (80ml) chicken stock
2 tablespoons redcurrant jelly

Melt butter in pan, add onions and bacon, cook, stirring, until onions are soft. Add cabbage, cook, stirring, until cabbage is just wilted. Stir in herbs; cool.

Layer pastry sheets together, brushing each with some of the extra butter. Spoon cabbage mixture down 1 long side of pastry, leaving 4cm border, top with eggs. Fold in sides, roll up firmly to enclose filling; brush with remaining extra butter, sprinkle with poppy seeds. Place strudel on greased oven tray. Bake in moderately hot oven about 30 minutes or until browned. Serve with apple sauce.

Apple Sauce Place apples and stock in small pan, cook, covered, about 5 minutes or until apples are soft; cool. Blend or process apple mixture until smooth, return to pan, add jelly, cook, stirring, until jelly is melted.

SERVES 4

Strudel can be prepared several hours ahead. Apple sauce can be made a day ahead.

Storage Covered, separately, in refrigerator
Freeze Not suitable
Microwave Apple sauce suitable

EGG AND BACON PIE

2 cups (320g) wholemeal plain flour
1 cup (150g) white plain flour
200g cold butter, chopped
1 egg
2 tablespoons iced water, approximately
10 bacon rashers, chopped
2 teaspoons olive oil
1 large (200g) onion, chopped
8 eggs, extra
2 cups (250g) grated tasty cheddar cheese
1/2 teaspoon seasoned pepper
1/4 cup chopped fresh chives
1 egg yolk

Grease deep 25cm round pie dish. Sift flours into bowl, rub in butter (or process flours and butter until mixture resembles breadcrumbs). Add egg and enough water to make ingredients cling together (or process until ingredients just come together). Press dough into a ball, knead on floured surface until smooth. Wrap in plastic, refrigerate 30 minutes.

Roll two-thirds of the pastry between sheets of baking paper until large enough to line prepared dish. Lift pastry carefully into dish, ease into side, trim edge. Lightly prick base with fork, cover, refrigerate 30 minutes.

Cover pastry with baking paper, fill with dried beans or rice, place on oven tray. Bake in moderately hot oven 10 minutes. Remove paper and beans carefully from pastry case, bake further 10 minutes or until browned, cool.

Bring large pan of water to boil, add bacon, return to boil, remove bacon; drain on absorbent paper. Heat oil in pan, add bacon and onion, cook, stirring, until onion is soft.

Break an extra egg into a cup, gently pour unbeaten egg into pastry case. Repeat with remaining eggs. Top with bacon mixture and combined cheese, pepper and chives.

Roll remaining pastry until large enough to cover pie. Brush edge of pie with egg yolk, carefully lift pastry onto pie, trim edge carefully. Decorate with pastry scraps, if desired; brush with egg yolk. Bake in moderate oven about 45 minutes or until browned.

SERVES 6 TO 8

Recipe can be made a day ahead.

Storage Covered, in refrigerator
Freeze Uncooked pastry suitable
Microwave Bacon and onion mixture suitable

Above left Pork and olive pastries
Left Cabbage, bacon and onion strudel
Below Egg and bacon pie

AUSSIE MEAT PIES

2 cups (300g) plain flour
125g lard, chopped
2 eggs, lightly beaten
1 tablespoon iced water,
  approximately
4 sheets ready-rolled puff pastry
1 egg yolk

FILLING
30g lard
2 medium (300g) onions, chopped
900g minced beef
1/4 cup (60ml) Worcestershire sauce
2 tablespoons soy sauce
2 teaspoons beef stock powder
1 1/2 cups (375g) water
1 teaspoon ground allspice
2 tablespoons cornflour
2 tablespoons water, extra

Sift flour into bowl rub in lard (or process flour and lard until mixture resembles breadcrumbs). Add eggs and enough water to make ingredients cling together (or process until ingredients just come together). Press dough into a ball, knead on floured surface until smooth. Wrap in plastic, refrigerate 30 minutes.

Divide dough into 8 portions. Roll each portion between sheets of baking paper until large enough to line 8 pie tins (1/2 cup/125ml capacity). Lift pastry into tins, ease into sides, trim edges. Lightly prick bases with fork, refrigerate 30 minutes.

Cover pastry cases with baking paper, fill with dried beans or rice, place tins on oven tray. Bake in moderately hot oven about 8 minutes. Remove paper and beans from pastry cases, bake further 8 minutes or until lightly browned; cool.

Make 8 tops by inverting a pie tin onto puff pastry, cut around edge with knife. Spoon cold filling into pastry cases, brush edges with a little egg yolk, gently press puff pastry tops into place. Decorate with pastry scraps, if desired. Brush pies with a little more egg yolk, return to oven trays. Bake in moderately hot oven about 20 minutes or until browned.

Filling Heat lard in pan, add onions, cook, stirring, until soft. Add mince, cook, stirring, until browned. Stir in sauces, stock powder, water and allspice, simmer, covered, 15 minutes. Stir in blended cornflour and extra water, stir over heat until mixture boils and thickens; cool.

MAKES 8

Recipe can be made a day ahead.

Storage Covered, in refrigerator
Freeze Suitable
Microwave Not suitable

LEEK AND HAM PIE WITH ORANGE CHIVE SAUCE

250g sliced ham
125g butter
2 medium (700g) leeks, sliced
10 sheets fillo pastry
2 tablespoons packaged breadcrumbs
1 cup (250ml) sour cream
2 tablespoons chopped fresh chives

ORANGE CHIVE SAUCE
1 medium (140g) lemon
2 medium (360g) oranges
2 tablespoons redcurrant jelly
1 tablespoon marsala
1/2 teaspoon French mustard
2 tablespoons chopped fresh chives

Grease 22cm pie plate. Cut ham into thin strips. Heat one-third of the butter in pan, add leeks, cook, stirring, until soft; drain. Brush pastry sheets with some

remaining melted butter, fold in half lengthways, brush with more butter. Overlap strips in plate, allowing strips to overhang edge.

Sprinkle pastry case with breadcrumbs. Place half the ham in pastry case, top with leeks. Spread combined sour cream and chives over leeks, top with remaining ham. Lift pastry edges towards centre to encase filling, pinch pastry together in centre, brush pastry with remaining butter. Bake pie in moderate

oven 25 minutes. Serve leek and ham pie with orange chive sauce.

Orange Chive Sauce Using vegetable peeler, peel rind thinly from lemon and 1 of the oranges. Cut rind into thin strips. Place rind in pan, cover with water, boil 3 minutes; drain. Squeeze juice from lemon and both oranges; you will need 2 tablespoons lemon juice and 1/2 cup (125ml) orange juice. Combine rind, juices, jelly, marsala and mustard in pan, bring to boil, simmer, uncovered, 2 minutes, stir in chives, cool.

SERVES 6

Recipe can be made a day ahead.

Storage Covered, in refrigerator
Freeze Not suitable
Microwave Sauce suitable

Left Aussie meat pies
Above Leek and ham pie with orange chive sauce

LAMB AND FETA PARCELS

1 tablespoon olive oil
4 large lamb fillets
1 medium (150g) onion,
finely chopped
2 cloves garlic, crushed
425g can tomatoes
1 tablespoon chopped fresh oregano
8 sheets fillo pastry
80g butter, melted
150g feta cheese, crumbled

Heat oil in pan, add lamb, cook over high heat until browned all over; drain on absorbent paper. Add onion and garlic to same pan, cook, stirring, until onion is soft. Add undrained crushed tomatoes and oregano, cook, uncovered, about 20 minutes, stirring occasionally, or until very thick; cool.

Layer 2 pastry sheets together, brushing each with butter. Place a piece of lamb at 1 end of pastry, top with quarter of the tomato mixture and quarter of the cheese, roll pastry around filling, tucking in ends, brush with a little more butter. Repeat with remaining pastry, butter, lamb, tomato mixture and cheese. Place parcels on greased oven tray. Bake in moderate oven about 20 minutes or until browned.

SERVES 4

Tomato mixture can be made a day ahead.

Storage Covered, in refrigerator
Freeze Not suitable
Microwave Not suitable

LAMB AND MUSHROOM PARCELS

40g butter
8 medium lamb fillets
4 sheets ready-rolled puff pastry
1 egg, lightly beaten

MUSHROOM FILLING
1 tablespoon olive oil
8 green shallots, chopped
150g button mushrooms, chopped
2 tablespoons drained chopped
sun-dried tomatoes
2 tablespoons chopped fresh parsley

Melt butter in pan, add lamb in batches, cook until browned; drain on absorbent paper. Stand lamb 10 minutes, cut each fillet in half.

Cut each sheet of pastry into 19cm squares. Pile 4 pieces of lamb in centre of each square; top with mushroom filling, press on lightly. Brush edges of pastry with egg, fold edges in to form a parcel.

Place parcels on greased oven trays, brush with remaining egg. Bake in moderately hot oven about 30 minutes or until pastry is puffed and browned.

Mushroom Filling Heat oil in pan, add shallots, cook, stirring, until soft. Add mushrooms, tomatoes and parsley, cook, stirring, until mushrooms are soft and liquid evaporated; cool.

SERVES 4

Recipe can be prepared a day ahead.

Storage Covered, in refrigerator
Freeze Uncooked lamb parcels suitable
Microwave Mushroom filling suitable

CURRIED BEEF PITHIVIER WITH MANGO SAMBAL

2 sheets ready-rolled puff pastry
1 egg yolk

FILLING
1 medium (200g) potato, chopped
1 tablespoon vegetable oil
1 medium (150g) onion, sliced
2 cloves garlic, crushed
2 teaspoons ground cumin
2 teaspoons ground coriander
500g minced beef
1 teaspoon beef stock powder

1/2 cup (35g) stale breadcrumbs
2 tablespoons shredded coconut
2 tablespoons currants
1/2 cup (125ml) plain yogurt

MANGO SAMBAL
2 medium (860g) mangoes, chopped
3 teaspoons mild sweet chilli sauce
1 tablespoon chopped fresh coriander

Cut a 21cm round from 1 sheet of pastry and a 23cm round from remaining sheet. Place smaller round on greased oven tray, top with filling, leaving 1cm border. Brush border with egg yolk, top with larger round of pastry, press edges together with fork. Brush with remaining egg yolk.

Using a sharp knife, mark pastry from centre to side; do not cut all the way through pastry. Bake in hot oven about 30 minutes or until browned and puffed. Serve with mango sambal.

Filling Boil, steam or microwave potato until just tender; drain. Heat oil in pan, add onion and garlic, cook, stirring, until onion is soft. Add cumin and coriander,

cook, stirring, until fragrant. Add mince, cook, stirring, until browned. Add stock powder, simmer, uncovered, until all liquid is evaporated. Add breadcrumbs, coconut, currants and potato; cool. Stir in yogurt.

Mango Sambal Combine all ingredients in bowl; mix well.

SERVES 4 TO 6

Recipe can be prepared a day ahead.

Storage Covered, in refrigerator
Freeze Uncooked pithivier suitable
Microwave Potato suitable

Above left Lamb and feta parcels
Left Lamb and mushroom parcels
Above Curried beef Pithivier with mango sambal

Vegetables

Transform vegetables into taste sensations as wide-ranging as a flaky vegetable pie, eggplant ricotta tarts with walnut pastry, French onion flan and much more. Vegetarian food is perfect for all occasions and seasons, and with the inclusion of eggs, pastry, sauces and fresh herbs and spices, vegetarian fare is as good for the budget as it is for health and nutrition.

ZUCCHINI AND FETA SPIRAL

2 tablespoons olive oil
1 medium (150g) onion, sliced
1 teaspoon ground caraway
3 medium (360g) zucchini,
  coarsely grated
1 medium (120g) carrot,
  coarsely grated
1 medium (200g) red pepper,
  chopped
250g feta cheese, crumbled
2 eggs, lightly beaten
14 sheets fillo pastry
125g butter, melted
1 egg, lightly beaten, extra
1 tablespoon grated
  parmesan cheese
1/2 teaspoon sesame seeds

TOMATO SAUCE
1 tablespoon olive oil
1 medium (150g) onion, sliced
2 cloves garlic, sliced
2 bay leaves
2 x 425g cans tomatoes
1 tablespoon tomato paste
1 teaspoon sugar
1/2 cup (125ml) water

Grease 31cm pizza pan. Heat oil in frying pan, add onion and caraway, cook, stirring, until onion is soft. Add zucchini, carrot and pepper, cook, stirring, until vegetables are soft and almost all liquid is evaporated. Remove from heat, stir in feta cheese; cool. Stir in eggs.

Layer 2 pastry sheets together, brushing each with butter. Spread 1/2 cup (125ml) vegetable mixture loosely down 1 long edge of pastry, leaving 3cm border at each end. Roll pastry lightly around mixture, tucking in ends. Brush roll with butter. Repeat with remaining pastry, butter and vegetable mixture.

Coil pastry rolls on pizza pan, starting from centre and working out to edge of pan to form a spiral, brushing sides of roll with extra egg as you work. Sprinkle with combined parmesan cheese and sesame seeds. Bake in moderately hot oven about 20 minutes or until browned. Serve with tomato sauce.

Tomato Sauce Heat oil in pan, add onion, garlic and bay leaves; cook, stirring, until onion is soft. Add undrained crushed tomatoes, paste, sugar and water, simmer, uncovered, about 25 minutes or until reduced by half. Discard bay leaves.

SERVES 6

Filling and sauce can be made a day ahead.

Storage Covered, separately, in refrigerator
Freeze Not suitable
Microwave Potatoes suitable

CREAMY CHEESE AND VEGETABLE GOUGERE

1½ quantities basic choux pastry;
   recipe page 113
1 tablespoon chopped fresh chives

FILLING
1 small (200g) leek
1 medium (120g) zucchini
1 medium (120g) carrot
1 medium (200g) red pepper
300ml cream
1¼ cups (160g) grated
   Swiss cheese
1 tablespoon chopped fresh oregano
1 tablespoon chopped fresh chives
200g button mushrooms, sliced
3 teaspoons cornflour
1½ tablespoons water

Make pastry according to directions on page 113. Grease shallow ovenproof dish (2 litre/8 cup capacity). Spread one-third of the pastry over base of dish.

Spoon remaining pastry into piping bag fitted with medium plain tube. Pipe pastry around edge of pastry base, leaving a hollow in the centre; bake in hot oven 10 minutes, reduce heat to moderately hot, bake further 45 minutes or until pastry is browned. Spoon hot filling into pastry case. Serve sprinkled with chives.

Filling Cut leek, zucchini, carrot and pepper into thin strips lengthways. Heat cream in pan, add cheese, stir until cheese is melted, stir in herbs. Add vegetables, cook, stirring, until just tender. Stir in blended cornflour and water, stir over heat until mixture boils and thickens slightly.

SERVES 4 TO 6

Recipe best made close to serving.

Freeze Not suitable
Microwave Not suitable

CARAWAY, POTATO AND MUSHROOM MINI PIES

1¹/₂ cups (225g) plain flour
³/₄ cup (105g) self-raising flour
1¹/₂ teaspoons, caraway seeds
50g cold butter, chopped
1 egg yolk
1 egg, lightly beaten
¹/₃ cup (80ml) iced water,
   approximately

FILLING
10 (400g) baby new potatoes,
   quartered
60g butter
2 medium (300g) onions, sliced
1 teaspoon caraway seeds
150g button mushrooms, chopped
¹/₄ cup (35g) plain flour
1¹/₂ cups (375ml) vegetable stock
1 teaspoon Dijon mustard
1 tablespoon chopped
   fresh rosemary
¹/₃ cup (25g) grated
   parmesan cheese

Grease 4 holes of Texas muffin pan (³/₄ cup/180ml capacity). Sift flours into bowl, add seeds, rub in butter. Add egg yolk, egg and enough water to make ingredients cling together. Press dough into a ball, knead gently on lightly floured surface until smooth. Wrap in plastic, refrigerate 30 minutes.

Divide two-thirds of the pastry into 4 portions. Roll each portion on lightly floured surface until 2mm thick, line prepared muffin holes, trim so pastry overhangs holes by 1cm. Brush overhanging edges with egg. Divide filling between pastry cases.

Roll out the remaining pastry, cut into 4 x 12cm rounds; place over filling, pinch edges together. Decorate with pastry shapes, if desired; brush pies with remaining egg. Bake in very hot oven 5 minutes, reduce heat to hot, bake further 25 minutes or until pies are browned.

Filling   Boil, steam or microwave potatoes until just tender; drain, cool. Heat butter in pan, add onions, cook, stirring, until soft. Add seeds and mushrooms, cook, stirring, 5 minutes. Stir in flour, stir over heat until bubbling.

Remove from heat, gradually stir in stock, simmer, uncovered, stirring occasionally, about 15 minutes. Stir in mustard, rosemary, cheese and potatoes; cool.

MAKES 4

Recipe best made a day ahead.

Storage Covered, in refrigerator
Freeze Not suitable
Microwave Potatoes suitable

Left Creamy cheese and vegetable gougere
Above Caraway, potato and mushroom
mini pies

PEPPER AND MUSHROOM SALAD WITH PESTO

3 sheets ready-rolled puff pastry
1 egg yolk
1 medium (200g) red pepper
1 medium (200g) yellow pepper
1 tablespoon olive oil
1 medium (120g) zucchini, sliced
1 small (230g) eggplant, sliced
3 cups (120g) mushrooms, sliced
1 medium (120g) carrot, sliced

PESTO
2 cups firmly packed fresh basil leaves
2 cloves garlic, crushed
1/4 cup (20g) grated parmesan cheese
2 tablespoons pine nuts, toasted
1/3 cup (80ml) extra virgin olive oil

Make base pattern by cutting 8cm x 12cm rectangle from paper. Make frame by cutting another 8cm x 12cm rectangle from paper. Inside this, cut a 5cm x 9cm rectangle, leaving 1.5cm border.

Using base pattern, cut 6 rectangles from 1 sheet of pastry. Place onto ungreased oven trays.

Brush 1 sheet of remaining pastry with water, top with remaining sheet of pastry; press to seal. Using frame pattern, cut 6 frame shapes from layered pastry; discard pastry scraps. Brush edges of

bases with water, press frames onto bases, forming shallow pastry cases.

Lightly prick bases with fork, cover, refrigerate 30 minutes. Brush tops of frames with egg yolk, bake in very hot oven about 10 minutes or until pastry is browned and puffed.

Cut peppers in half, remove seeds and membranes; cut each half into 6 pieces lengthways. Heat griddle pan, brush with oil, add vegetables in batches, cook until tender. Fill hot pastry cases with hot vegetables, drizzle with pesto.

Pesto Blend or process basil, garlic, cheese and nuts until finely chopped. Gradually add oil while motor is operating, process until smooth.

SERVES 6

Unbaked pastry cases and pesto can be prepared a day ahead.

Storage Pastry, in airtight container. Pesto, covered on surface with plastic wrap, in refrigerator
Freeze Uncooked pastry cases and pesto suitable
Microwave Not suitable

PEAR AND ROQUEFORT TARTLETS

1 quantity basic shortcrust pastry; recipe page 112
1 medium (180g) pear, peeled, cored
50g butter
3 medium (450g) onions, thinly sliced
2 teaspoons red wine vinegar
30g butter, extra
2 tablespoons walnuts, chopped, toasted
75g roquefort cheese, crumbled
1 witlof
1 bunch (170g) rocket
1 red coral lettuce

DRESSING
1/3 cup (80ml) olive oil
2 tablespoons red wine vinegar
1 teaspoon walnut oil

Grease 4 x 12cm round loose-base tartlet tins. Make pastry according to directions on page 112.

Divide pastry into 4 portions. Roll each portion between sheets of baking paper until large enough to line prepared tins. Lift pastry into tins, ease into sides, trim edges, lightly prick bases with fork. Cut 4 small pear shapes from pastry scraps. Place tins and pear cut-outs on oven tray; cover, refrigerate 30 minutes.

Cover pastry cases with baking paper, fill with dried beans or rice. Bake cases and pear shapes in moderately hot oven 10 minutes. Remove paper and beans

CARROT AND LENTIL FLAN

1 quantity basic wholemeal pastry; recipe page 112
1/2 cup (100g) red lentils
3 medium (360g) carrots, thinly sliced
2 tablespoons olive oil
1 medium (150g) onion, finely chopped
2 cloves garlic, crushed
1 stick celery, chopped
3 eggs, lightly beaten
1/2 cup (125ml) vegetable stock
1/2 cup (125ml) cream
2 tablespoons grated parmesan cheese
2 tablespoons chopped fresh chives
1 tablespoon chopped fresh parsley

Make pastry according to directions on page 112. Roll pastry between sheets of baking paper until large enough to line deep 24cm round loose-base flan tin. Lift pastry into tin, ease into side, trim edge. Lightly prick base with fork, refrigerate 30 minutes.

Cover pastry with baking paper, fill with dried beans or rice, place on oven tray. Bake in moderately hot oven 10 minutes. Remove paper and beans carefully from pastry case, bake further 10 minutes or until browned; cool.

Add lentils to pan of boiling water, boil, uncovered, about 8 minutes or until lentils are tender; drain, cool 10 minutes. Blend or process lentils until smooth. Boil, steam or microwave carrots until just tender; drain.

Heat oil in pan, add onion, garlic and celery, cook, stirring, until onion is soft. Add carrots, cook, stirring, further 5 minutes; cool. Spoon vegetable mixture into prepared pastry case.

Combine lentil puree, eggs, stock, cream, cheese and herbs in bowl; mix well. Pour lentil mixture over carrot mixture, bake in moderately hot oven about 35 minutes or until set.

SERVES 4 TO 6

Recipe can be made a day ahead.

Storage Covered, in refrigerator
Freeze Uncooked pastry suitable
Microwave Lentils and carrots suitable

carefully from pastry cases, bake further 15 minutes or until pastries are browned.

Cut pear into quarters, slice lengthways keeping tops intact. Gently press slices into a fan shape. Melt butter in pan, add onions, cook, stirring, over low heat about 15 minutes or until onions are very soft. Stir in vinegar, remove from pan; cool. Melt extra butter in same pan, add fanned pears, cook gently on both sides until lightly browned and just tender.

Divide onion mixture between pastry cases, top with nuts, cheese and pears. Bake in moderately hot oven about 15 minutes or until cheese is melted, top

with pastry pears. Serve with combined torn salad leaves, drizzle with dressing.

Dressing Combine all ingredients in jar; shake well.

SERVES 4

Recipe can be made a day ahead.

Storage Airtight container
Freeze Uncooked pastry suitable
Microwave Not suitable

Far left Pepper and mushroom salad with pesto
Above left Carrot and lentil flan
Left Pear and roquefort tartlets

VEGETABLE AND PESTO PIE WITH RED PEPPER SAUCE

2 medium (700g) eggplants, thinly sliced
coarse cooking salt
1/4 cup (60ml) olive oil
4 medium (800g) red peppers
1 bunch (650g) English spinach
1/2 cup (65g) drained, sliced sun-dried tomatoes
24 small drained artichoke hearts, halved
150g feta cheese, crumbled

PASTRY
3 cups (450g) plain flour
2 teaspoons (7g) dried yeast
1 1/2 teaspoons sugar
1 1/2 tablespoons olive oil
1 cup (250ml) warm water, approximately

PESTO
2 cups firmly packed fresh basil leaves
1/3 cup (50g) pine nuts
2 cloves garlic, crushed
1/3 cup (80ml) olive oil
1/4 cup (20g) grated parmesan cheese

RED PEPPER SAUCE
30g butter
1 medium (150g) onion, finely chopped
1 large (350g) red pepper, finely chopped
1 tablespoon plain flour
1 cup (250ml) vegetable stock
1/2 cup (125ml) cream

Grease deep 24.5cm round loose-base flan tin. Place eggplant slices on wire rack (or in colander), sprinkle with salt, stand 30 minutes. Rinse slices under cold water; drain on absorbent paper. Heat oil in pan, add eggplant in batches, cook until lightly browned; drain eggplant slices on absorbent paper.

Quarter peppers, remove seeds and membranes. Grill peppers, skin side up, until skin blisters and blackens. Peel away skin. Boil, steam or microwave spinach until just wilted; drain, rinse under cold water, drain, pat spinach dry with absorbent paper.

Roll two-thirds of the pastry on floured surface until large enough to line prepared tin. Lift pastry into tin, ease into side, trim edge. Layer eggplant slices, tomatoes, spinach, artichokes, cheese, pesto and peppers in pastry case. Roll remaining pastry until large enough to cover tin, brush edge with water, place pastry on top, press edges together; trim edge. Decorate with pastry scraps, if desired. Cut 3 slits in pastry. Bake in moderately hot oven about 40 minutes or until browned. Cool in tin, refrigerate overnight. Serve with red pepper sauce.

Pastry Sift flour into bowl, stir in yeast, sugar, oil and enough water to mix to a firm dough. Knead about 5 minutes on floured surface until smooth and elastic.

Pesto Blend or process all ingredients until smooth.

Red Pepper Sauce Melt butter in pan, add onion and pepper, cook, stirring, until onion is soft. Add flour, stir over heat 1 minute. Remove from heat, gradually stir in combined stock and cream, stir over heat until mixture boils and thickens. Blend or process sauce until smooth, strain; cool, cover, refrigerate.

SERVES 6 TO 8

Recipe can be made 2 days ahead.

Storage Covered, in refrigerator
Freeze Not suitable
Microwave Spinach suitable

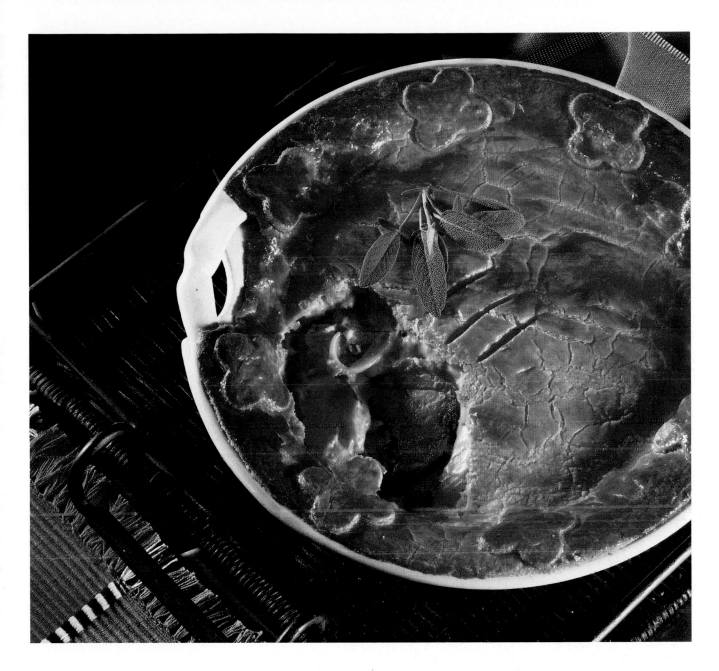

POTATO AND BLUE VEIN CHEESE PIE

1¹/₂ quantities basic shortcrust
   pastry; recipe page 112
¹/₄ cup (60ml) olive oil
6 medium (1.2kg) potatoes, sliced
60g butter
1 medium (150g) onion, sliced
¹/₄ cup (35g) plain flour
1³/₄ cups (430ml) milk
¹/₂ teaspoon dry mustard
1 teaspoon chopped fresh thyme
100g blue vein cheese, crumbled
1 egg yolk

Grease 28cm pie dish (1.5 litre/6 cup capacity). Make pastry according to directions on page 112. Roll two-thirds of the pastry between sheets of baking paper until large enough to line prepared dish. Lift pastry into dish, ease into side, trim edge. Lightly prick base with fork, refrigerate 30 minutes.

Cover pastry with baking paper, fill with dried beans or rice, place on oven tray. Bake in moderately hot oven 15 minutes. Remove paper and beans carefully from pastry case, bake further 15 minutes or until lightly browned; cool.

Heat oil in pan, add potatoes in batches, cook until lightly browned and tender; drain on absorbent paper, cool.

Melt butter in pan, add onion, cook, stirring, until soft. Add flour, stir over heat until bubbling. Remove from heat, gradually stir in milk, stir over heat until mixture boils and thickens. Remove from heat, stir in mustard and thyme.

Layer potato, cheese and sauce in pastry case. Roll remaining pastry until large enough to cover top of dish, brush edge with some of the egg yolk. Place pastry on top, press edges together firmly; trim edge. Decorate with pastry scraps, if desired. Brush pie with remaining egg yolk, cut 3 slits in pastry, bake in moderately hot oven about 40 minutes or until browned.

SERVES 6

Recipe can be made a day ahead.

Storage Covered, in refrigerator
Freeze Not suitable
Microwave Not suitable

Left Vegetable and pesto pie with red pepper sauce
Above Potato and blue vein cheese pie

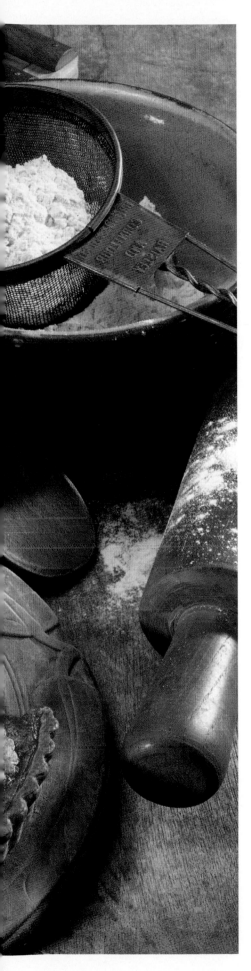

OPEN RATATOUILLE PIE

2¹/₄ cups (335g) plain flour
200g cold butter, chopped
3 egg yolks
2 tablespoons iced water,
   approximately

RATATOUILLE FILLING
1 large (500g) eggplant
coarse cooking salt
2 tablespoons olive oil
1 medium (150g) onion, sliced
1 clove garlic, crushed
2 medium (240g) zucchini, sliced
¹/₂ medium (100g) red
   pepper, chopped
¹/₂ medium (100g) green
   pepper, chopped
425g can tomatoes
1 tablespoon tomato paste
1 teaspoon sugar
1 medium (130g) tomato, chopped
1 tablespoon chopped fresh oregano
2 tablespoons chopped fresh thyme
2 tablespoons stale breadcrumbs

Sift flour into bowl, rub in butter (or process flour and butter until mixture resembles breadcrumbs). Add 2 of the egg yolks and enough water to make ingredients cling together (or process until ingredients just come together). Press dough into a ball, knead gently on lightly floured surface until smooth. Wrap in plastic, refrigerate 30 minutes.

Roll pastry between sheets of baking paper until large enough to line 25cm pie dish (1.25 litre/5 cup capacity) and overhang edge by about 8cm. Spoon in ratatouille filling, fold overhanging pastry over filling, leaving a gap in the centre. Brush pastry with remaining egg yolk, bake in hot oven about 40 minutes or until pastry is browned.

Ratatouille Filling Cut eggplant into 2cm pieces, place in colander, sprinkle with salt, stand 30 minutes. Rinse under cold water, drain on absorbent paper.

Heat oil in pan, add onion and garlic, cook, stirring, until onion is soft. Add eggplant, zucchini and peppers, cook, stirring, 3 minutes. Add undrained crushed canned tomatoes, paste, sugar and fresh tomato, simmer, uncovered about 10 minutes or until mixture thickens. Add herbs, cook, stirring, 3 minutes; cool. Stir in breadcrumbs.

SERVES 4

Recipe can be made a day ahead.

Storage Covered, in refrigerator
Freeze Not suitable
Microwave Not suitable

From left Open ratatouille pie; French onion flan

FRENCH ONION FLAN

1¹/₄ cups (185g) plain flour
80g cold butter, chopped
¹/₂ cup (40g) grated
   parmesan cheese
1 teaspoon ground coriander
2 teaspoons seeded mustard
2 tablespoons iced water,
   approximately
¹/₂ cup (40g) grated parmesan
   cheese, extra

FILLING
1 tablespoon olive oil
30g butter
4 medium (680g) red Spanish
   onions, sliced
1 tablespoon red wine vinegar
2 teaspoons brown sugar
3 eggs, lightly beaten
¹/₃ cup (80ml) cream

Sift flour into bowl, rub in butter, cheese, coriander and mustard (or process ingredients until mixture resembles breadcrumbs). Add enough water to make ingredients cling together (or process until ingredients just come together). Press dough into a ball, knead gently on lightly floured surface until smooth. Wrap in plastic, refrigerate 30 minutes.

Roll three-quarters of the pastry between sheets of baking paper until large enough to line 24cm round loose-base flan tin. Lift pastry into tin, ease into side, trim edge, reserve pastry scraps. Lightly prick base with fork, refrigerate 30 minutes.

Combine reserved pastry scraps with remaining pastry, roll between sheets of baking paper until 2mm thick. Cut pastry into 14 x 15cm rounds.

Cover pastry case with baking paper, fill with dried beans or rice, place on oven tray. Bake in moderately hot oven 10 minutes. Remove paper and beans carefully from pastry case, bake further 10 minutes or until lightly browned; cool.

Sprinkle extra cheese over base of pastry case, carefully spoon filling over cheese, top with pastry rounds. Bake in moderate oven about 40 minutes or until filling is set.

Filling Heat oil and butter in pan, add onions, cook, stirring, until onions are very soft. Stir in vinegar and sugar, cook, stirring, until sugar is dissolved; cool. Combine eggs and cream in bowl, whisk until combined, stir in onion mixture.

SERVES 6 TO 8

Recipe can be made a day ahead.

Storage Covered, in refrigerator
Freeze Uncooked pastry suitable
Microwave Not suitable

Desserts

All the scrumptious pastry desserts you ever wanted to make (plus many you've never even thought of!) are included in this spectacular array of delights sure to suit any occasion. Fresh fruit, devilish chocolate and caramel and refreshing citrus flavours, are included among the many delicious tarts, strudels, pies and flans – all perfectly wicked indulgences.

PLUM AND ALMOND TART

1 cup (150g) plain flour
1/4 cup (35g) self-raising flour
2 tablespoons custard powder
1 tablespoon icing sugar mixture
3/4 cup (90g) packaged
   ground almonds
90g cold butter, chopped
1 tablespoon iced water,
   approximately
825g can dark plums in light
   syrup, drained

FILLING
1/4 cup (35g) plain flour
2 tablespoons self-raising flour
1/4 teaspoon ground nutmeg
1/4 teaspoon ground cinnamon
1/4 cup (55g) caster sugar
3 eggs, lightly beaten
1 1/2 cups (375ml) milk

Grease deep 24cm round loose-base flan tin. Sift flours, custard powder and sugar into bowl, stir in nuts, rub in butter (or process ingredients until mixture resembles breadcrumbs). Add enough water to make ingredients cling together (or process until mixture just comes together). Press dough into a ball, knead gently on floured surface until smooth. Wrap in plastic, refrigerate 30 minutes.

Roll pastry between sheets of baking paper until large enough to line prepared tin. Lift pastry into tin, ease into side, trim edge. Lightly prick base with fork, refrigerate 30 minutes.

Cover pastry with baking paper, fill with dried beans or rice, place on oven tray. Bake in moderately hot oven 10 minutes. Remove paper and beans carefully from pastry case, bake further 10 minutes or until lightly browned; cool.

Cut plums in half, discard seeds, place plums in pastry case. Pour filling over plums, bake in moderate oven about 1 hour or until firm. Serve warm, dusted with sifted icing sugar, if desired.

Filling Combine sifted flours, spices and sugar in bowl, gradually stir in eggs, then milk; mix to a smooth batter.

SERVES 8

Recipe best made close to serving.

Freeze Uncooked pastry suitable
Microwave Not suitable

APPLE AND PEAR STRUDEL

2 large (400g) apples
2 medium (360g) pears
1/2 cup (110g) caster sugar
1 teaspoon vanilla essence
1/4 teaspoon ground nutmeg
1 teaspoon ground cinnamon
1 teaspoon grated lemon rind
3/4 cup (120g) sultanas
30g butter
1 cup (70g) stale breadcrumbs
1/2 cup (100g) firmly packed
   brown sugar
125g butter, melted, extra

STRUDEL PASTRY
1 1/2 cups (225g) plain flour
1 egg, lightly beaten
1 tablespoon vegetable oil
1/3 cup (80ml) warm water

Peel and core apples and pears; slice very thinly, using a vegetable peeler. Combine fruit, caster sugar and essence in bowl; mix well. Cover, stand 1 hour.

Drain as much excess liquid from fruit mixture as possible. Combine fruit mixture with spices, rind and sultanas in bowl; mix lightly. Heat butter in pan, add breadcrumbs, stir over low heat until breadcrumbs are golden brown; cool. Combine breadcrumbs and brown sugar in bowl; mix well.

Strudel Pastry Sift flour into bowl, make well in centre of flour, add egg and oil. Gradually add water, mixing to a soft dough with hand.

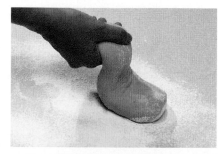

Turn dough onto lightly floured surface; knead into a ball. Pick up dough and throw it down on lightly floured surface; do this about 100 times.

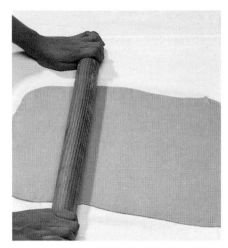

Knead again for 5 minutes. The more the dough is thrown down and kneaded, the lighter it will be. Knead dough into a ball and place in lightly oiled bowl, cover, stand in warm place 45 minutes. Cover large surface with large clean cloth, rub flour over surface. Roll out dough as thinly as possible.

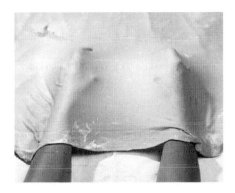

Flour back of hands, slip them under dough, then start stretching dough gently from centre. Continue stretching dough until it is paper thin and approximately 72cm square.

Brush pastry with some of the extra butter. Sprinkle breadcrumb mixture over

half the pastry. Spoon fruit mixture along 1 end of pastry about 5cm from edge. Fold in sides of pastry to edge of filling. Gather cloth in hands and carefully roll up strudel, using the cloth as a guide.

Place strudel on large greased oven tray, curving gently and carefully into horseshoe shape. Brush with more butter. Bake in moderately hot oven about 35 minutes or until golden brown. When cold, dust with sifted icing sugar. Serve with cream, if desired.

SERVES 8

Recipe can be made a day ahead.

Storage Airtight container
Freeze Not suitable
Microwave Not suitable

MANGO CREAM TARTLETS WITH APRICOT GLAZE

1 quantity basic biscuit pastry; recipe page 113
1 medium (430g) mango, sliced
3 medium (270g) kiwi fruit, sliced

MANGO CREAM
1 small (300g) mango, chopped
300ml thickened cream
1 tablespoon icing sugar mixture

APRICOT GLAZE
¹/₂ cup (125ml) apricot jam
1 tablespoon water

Make pastry according to directions on page 113. Divide pastry into 6 portions. Roll each portion between sheets of floured baking paper until large enough to line 6 x 12.5cm round loose-base flan tins. Lift pastry into tins, ease into sides, trim edges. Lightly prick bases with fork, refrigerate 30 minutes.

Cover pastry cases with baking paper, fill with dried beans or rice, place on oven tray. Bake in moderately hot oven 10 minutes. Remove paper and beans carefully from pastry cases. Bake further 10 minutes or until lightly browned; cool.

Divide mango cream between pastry cases, top with sliced mango and kiwi fruit; brush with apricot glaze.

Mango Cream Blend or process mango until smooth. Beat cream and sifted icing sugar in small bowl until firm peaks form, fold in pureed mango.

Apricot Glaze Heat jam and water in small pan; strain.

MAKES 6

Pastry cases can be made 3 days ahead. Filling can be made a day ahead. Assemble just before serving.

Storage Pastry cases, in airtight container. Filling, covered, in refrigerator
Freeze Uncooked pastry suitable
Microwave Glaze suitable

Left Apple and pear strudel
Below Mango cream tartlets with apricot glaze

LIME AND BUTTERMILK PIE

**1 quantity basic shortcrust pastry;
recipe page 112**

FILLING
**2 eggs
1/2 cup (110g) caster sugar
2 tablespoons plain flour
1/4 cup (60ml) buttermilk
2 teaspoons grated lime rind
3 teaspoons lime juice**

Make pastry according to directions on page 112. Roll pastry between sheets of baking paper until large enough to line 24cm round loose-base flan tin. Lift pastry into tin, ease into side, trim edge. Prick base with fork, refrigerate 30 minutes.

Cover pastry with baking paper, fill with dried beans or rice, place on oven tray. Bake in moderately hot oven 10 minutes. Remove paper and beans from pastry case, bake further 10 minutes or until lightly browned; cool. Pour filling into pastry case, bake in moderate oven 20 minutes, reduce heat to moderately slow, bake further 20 minutes or until filling is set. Dust with sifted icing sugar, if desired.

Filling Beat eggs and sugar in small bowl with electric mixer until thick and creamy. Fold in remaining ingredients.

SERVES 6

Recipe can be made a day ahead.

Storage Covered, in refrigerator
Freeze Uncooked pastry suitable
Microwave Not suitable

APPLE GALETTE

We used a combination of Granny Smith and red-skinned apples in this recipe.

**500g packet ready-rolled puff
pastry roll
4 large (800g) apples, cored
2 tablespoons lemon juice
1 tablespoon caster sugar
60g butter, chopped
2 tablespoons apricot jam,
warmed, sieved**

Cut a 35cm length from puff pastry roll, place on oven tray. Turn edges in about 2cm, press lightly. Thinly slice whole apples, toss in juice, place apples on pastry. Sprinkle with sugar, dot with half the butter.

Preheat oven to highest temperature, place galette in oven, reduce to moderately hot. Bake 20 minutes, dot with remaining butter, bake further 25 minutes or until browned. Brush hot galette with jam. Serve warm or cold with whipped cream, if desired.

SERVES 6

Recipe can be made a day ahead.

Storage Covered, in refrigerator
Freeze Not suitable
Microwave Not suitable

Below Lime and buttermilk pie
Right Apple galette

PEAR DUMPLINGS WITH BUTTERSCOTCH SAUCE

4 medium (720g) firm pears
1 cup (250ml) water
1 cup (250ml) dry white wine
1 cup (220g) caster sugar
5cm strip orange rind
5cm strip lemon rind
1 cinnamon stick
1/4 teaspoon ground cinnamon
1 teaspoon caster sugar, extra
375g packet puff pastry
1 egg, lightly beaten

BUTTERSCOTCH SAUCE
40g butter
1/3 cup (65g) brown sugar
3/4 cup (180ml) thickened cream

Peel pears, leaving stems intact. Combine water, wine, sugar, rinds and cinnamon stick in pan, stir over heat until sugar is dissolved. Add pears, simmer, covered, about 15 minutes or until pears are just tender, turning occasionally. Transfer pears and liquid to bowl; cool. Cover, refrigerate overnight.

Remove pears from liquid; pat dry with absorbent paper. Sprinkle the pears with combined ground cinnamon and extra sugar.

Roll pastry to approximately 40cm square, cut into 4 squares. Place a pear in centre of each square. Lightly brush edges of pastry with egg. Pull pastry ends to encase pear, press pastry firmly onto pear. Brush pastry with more egg, place pears on greased oven tray. Preheat oven to highest temperature, place pears in oven, reduce temperature to hot, bake about 40 minutes or until pastry is browned. Serve with butterscotch sauce.

Butterscotch Sauce Combine all ingredients in pan, stir over heat, without boiling, until sugar is dissolved. Simmer, uncovered, without stirring, about 5 minutes or until slightly thickened.

SERVES 4

Pears and butterscotch sauce can be prepared a day ahead.

Storage Covered, separately, in refrigerator
Freeze Not suitable
Microwave Not suitable

Left Pear dumplings with butterscotch sauce
Right Caramelised apple and saffron tartlets

CARAMELISED APPLE AND SAFFRON TARTLETS

**1 quantity basic pate sucree;
recipe page 113**
3 small (390g) apples
2 tablespoons water
¹/₂ cup (125ml) honey
³/₄ cup (180ml) thickened cream
2 tablespoons honey, extra
1 tablespoon caster sugar
2 egg yolks
6 saffron strands

Make pastry according to directions on page 113. Divide pastry into 6 portions. Roll each portion between sheets of lightly floured baking paper until large enough to line 6 deep 10cm round loose-base flan tins. Lift pastry into tins, ease into sides, trim edges. Lightly prick pastry with fork, refrigerate 30 minutes.

Cover pastry cases with baking paper, fill with dried beans or rice, place on oven trays. Bake in moderately hot oven 10 minutes. Remove paper and beans carefully from pastry cases, bake further 10 minutes or until browned; cool.

Peel, core and halve apples, slice apples lengthways without cutting all the way through. Heat water and honey in pan, add apples curved side down, cook until apples begin to soften. Turn apples, bring to boil, constantly spoon boiling honey mixture over apples until just tender and browned; cool on wire rack.

Combine cream, extra honey, sugar, egg yolks and saffron in bowl; whisk until smooth. Place an apple half into each pastry case, pour over cream mixture. Bake in moderately slow oven about 40 minutes, or until filling is just set.

MAKES 6

Recipe can be made 3 hours ahead.

Storage Covered, in refrigerator
Freeze Uncooked pastry suitable
Microwave Not suitable

BEST EVER
LEMON MERINGUE PIE

1 quantity basic pate sucree; recipe page 113

FILLING
¹/₂ cup (75g) cornflour
1 cup (220g) caster sugar
¹/₂ cup (125ml) lemon juice
1¹/₄ cups (310ml) water
2 teaspoons grated lemon rind
3 egg yolks
60g butter

MERINGUE
4 egg whites
pinch cream of tartar
¹/₂ cup (110g) caster sugar

Make pastry according to directions on page 113. Roll pastry between sheets of lightly floured baking paper until large enough to line 24cm round loose-base flan tin. Lift pastry into tin, ease into side, trim edge. Lightly prick pastry with fork, refrigerate 30 minutes.

Cover pastry with baking paper, fill with dried beans or rice, place on oven tray. Bake in moderately hot oven 10 minutes. Remove paper and beans carefully from pastry case, bake further 10 minutes or until lightly browned; cool to room temperature.

Spread filling into pastry case, top with meringue; spread to edge of pastry. Bake in moderate oven about 5 minutes or until meringue is lightly browned. Stand 5 minutes before serving.

Filling Combine cornflour and sugar in pan, gradually blend in juice and water, stir until smooth. Stir over heat until mixture boils and thickens (mixture should be very thick). Reduce heat, simmer, stirring vigorously, for 30 seconds. Remove from heat, quickly stir in rind, yolks and butter, stir until butter is melted; cover, cool.

Meringue Beat egg whites in bowl with electric mixer until soft peaks form, add cream of tartar. Gradually add sugar, beat until dissolved between additions.

SERVES 6 TO 8

Pastry case and filling can be made a day ahead. Meringue best made just before serving.

RHUBARB MERINGUE PIES

**1 quantity basic pate sucree; recipe
page 113**

FILLING
500g chopped fresh rhubarb
¹/₂ cup (110g) sugar
¹/₃ cup (80ml) water
pinch ground ginger
2 egg yolks
¹/₄ cup (60ml) cream

MERINGUE TOPPING
3 egg whites
¹/₂ cup (110g) caster sugar

Make pastry according to directions on page 113. Divide pastry into 4 portions, roll each portion between sheets of floured baking paper until large enough to line 4 x 11.5cm round loose-base flan tins. Lift pastry into tins, trim edges. Lightly prick bases with fork, refrigerate 30 minutes.

Cover pastry with baking paper, fill with dried beans or rice, place on oven tray. Bake in moderately hot oven 10 minutes. Remove paper and beans carefully from pastry cases, bake further 10 minutes or until lightly browned; cool. Spoon filling into pastry cases, bake in moderate oven about 30 minutes or until filling is firm. Spread meringue topping over rhubarb mixture, bake pies in moderate oven about 5 minutes or until lightly browned.

Filling Combine rhubarb, sugar, water and ginger in pan, simmer, uncovered, about 3 minutes or until rhubarb is tender, drain in plastic strainer; cool in strainer. Combine rhubarb mixture, egg yolks and cream in bowl; mix well.

Meringue Topping Beat egg whites and sugar in small bowl with electric mixer until sugar is dissolved and firm peaks form.

MAKES 4

Pastry cases can be made 3 days ahead.

Storage Airtight container
Freeze Uncooked pastry suitable
Microwave Not suitable

Storage Pastry case, in airtight container. Filling, covered, in refrigerator
Freeze Uncooked pastry suitable
Microwave Not suitable

Above Best ever lemon meringue pie
Right Rhubarb meringue pies

RICH CARAMEL CREAM TART

**1 quantity basic shortcrust pastry;
recipe page 112**
**1 cup (80g) flaked
almonds, toasted**
60g dark chocolate, grated

FILLING
90g butter, chopped
**3/4 cup (150g) firmly packed
brown sugar**
1/2 cup (125ml) water
1/3 cup (50g) cornflour
1/2 cup (125ml) milk
1/4 cup (60ml) thickened cream
2 egg yolks

TOPPING
2/3 cup (160ml) thickened cream
1/4 teaspoon almond essence
1 tablespoon icing sugar mixture
125g ricotta cheese

Grease 24cm round loose-base flan tin. Make pastry according to directions on page 112. Roll pastry between sheets of baking paper until large enough to line prepared tin. Lift pastry into tin, ease into side, trim edge. Lightly prick base with fork, refrigerate 30 minutes.

Cover pastry with baking paper, fill with dried beans or rice, place on oven tray. Bake in moderately hot oven 10 minutes. Remove paper and beans carefully from pastry, bake further 15 minutes or until lightly browned; cool.

Spread filling into pastry case, cover, refrigerate several hours or overnight. Just before serving, spread topping over filling, decorate with nuts and chocolate.

Filling Combine butter with sugar in heavy-base pan, stir over low heat, without boiling, until sugar is dissolved, boil, stirring occasionally, about 5 minutes or until mixture is golden brown.

Add water, stir until all pieces of caramel are melted. Stir in blended cornflour and milk, stir over heat until mixture boils and thickens, continue stirring 2 minutes or until very thick; cool 10 minutes. Transfer mixture to small bowl, stir in cream, then yolks, beat with electric mixer until smooth; cover, cool.

Topping Beat cream, essence and sifted icing sugar in small bowl until firm peaks form. Gently fold cream mixture into ricotta in 2 batches.

SERVES 8

Tart can be made a day ahead.

Storage Covered, in refrigerator
Freeze Uncooked pastry suitable
Microwave Not suitable

BANANA AND STRAWBERRY TARTLETS

1 1/2 cups (225g) plain flour
2/3 cup (60g) coconut, toasted
150g cold butter, chopped
**1 1/2 tablespoons iced water,
approximately**
250g strawberries, halved
**2 tablespoons strawberry jam,
warmed, sieved**
1/3 cup (15g) flaked coconut

FILLING
1 1/2 tablespoons custard powder
1/4 cup (55g) caster sugar
3/4 cup (180ml) milk
1 small (130g) ripe banana
1/3 cup (80ml) thickened cream

Sift flour into bowl, stir in toasted coconut, rub in butter (or process dry ingredients and butter until mixture resembles breadcrumbs). Add enough water to make ingredients cling together (or process until ingredients just come together). Press dough into a ball, knead gently on lightly floured surface until smooth. Wrap in plastic, refrigerate 30 minutes.

Divide pastry into 4 portions, roll each portion between sheets of baking paper until large enough to line 4 x 11.5cm round loose-base flan tins. Lift pastry into tins, ease into sides, trim edges. Lightly prick bases with fork, refrigerate 30 minutes.

Cover pastry with baking paper, fill with dried beans or rice, place on oven tray. Bake in moderately hot oven 10 minutes. Remove paper and beans carefully from pastry cases, bake further 10 minutes or until lightly browned; cool.

Just before serving, spoon filling into pastry cases, top with strawberries. Lightly brush strawberries with jam, sprinkle with flaked coconut.

Filling Combine custard powder and sugar in pan, gradually blend in milk, stir over heat until custard boils and thickens. Blend or process custard and banana until smooth, transfer mixture to bowl, cover surface with plastic wrap; refrigerate until cold. Beat cream in small bowl until firm peaks form. Gently fold cream into banana mixture.

MAKES 4

Pastry cases can be made 3 days ahead.

Storage Airtight container
Freeze Uncooked pastry suitable
Microwave Not suitable

Left Banana and strawberry tartlets
Above Rich caramel cream tart

APPLE HAZELNUT TART

1 quantity basic shortcrust pastry; recipe page 112
¼ cup (25g) ground hazelnuts
2 large (400g) apples, peeled, sliced
2 tablespoons caster sugar
½ cup (125ml) thickened cream
2 eggs, lightly beaten
1 tablespoon milk
½ teaspoon grated lemon rind
¼ teaspoon ground nutmeg

GLAZE
¼ cup (60ml) apricot jam
½ teaspoon brandy

Make pastry according to directions on page 112. Roll pastry between sheets of baking paper until large enough to line 24cm round loose-base flan tin. Lift pastry into tin, ease into side, trim edge. Lightly prick base with fork, refrigerate 30 minutes.

Sprinkle nuts into pastry case, top with apples, then sugar. Bake in moderately hot oven 40 minutes or until apples are just tender. Pour combined cream, eggs, milk, rind and nutmeg over apples, bake in moderate oven 20 minutes or until set. Cool 10 minutes, brush with glaze. Serve with whipped cream, if desired.

Glaze Warm jam and brandy in pan, stirring; strain.

SERVES 6

Recipe can be made a day ahead.

Storage Covered, in refrigerator
Freeze Uncooked pastry suitable
Microwave Not suitable

WARM BERRY COMPOTE

¾ cup (180ml) water
¾ cup (180ml) dry red wine
¼ cup (55g) caster sugar
1 cinnamon stick
250g strawberries, halved
150g blueberries
150g raspberries
150g boysenberries
4 sheets ready-rolled puff pastry
1 egg yolk
1 teaspoon milk

Combine water, wine, sugar and cinnamon in pan, stir over heat, without boiling, until sugar is dissolved. Boil, uncovered, without stirring, until liquid is reduced to 1 cup (250ml). Reduce heat, add fruit, simmer, uncovered, 3 minutes. Remove from heat, discard cinnamon. Spoon into 4 ovenproof dishes (2 cup/500ml capacity), place dishes onto oven tray.

Cut a 17cm round from each pastry sheet, cut out centres with 7cm cutter. Brush edges of dishes with combined egg yolk and milk, place pastry rounds onto dishes, press down firmly. Decorate with pastry scraps, if desired, brush tops with remaining egg yolk mixture. Preheat oven to highest temperature, place dishes in oven, reduce to moderately hot, bake about 25 minutes or until browned.

MAKES 4

Recipe can be made a day ahead.

Storage Covered, in refrigerator
Freeze Not suitable
Microwave Not suitable

CHERRY CLAFOUTI

500g fresh ripe cherries
1 quantity basic biscuit pastry; recipe page 113
⅓ cup (80ml) milk
⅓ cup (80ml) thickened cream
½ vanilla bean, split
3 eggs
½ cup (110g) caster sugar
¼ teaspoon cornflour
1 tablespoon Kirsch
1 tablespoon caster sugar, extra

Remove stones from cherries. Make pastry according to directions on page 113. Roll pastry between sheets of floured baking paper until large enough to line 24cm round loose-base flan tin. Lift pastry into tin, ease into side, trim edge. Lightly prick base with fork, refrigerate 30 minutes.

Cover pastry with baking paper, fill with dried beans or rice, place on oven tray. Bake in moderately hot oven 10 minutes. Remove paper and beans carefully from pastry case, bake further 10 minutes or until lightly browned; cool.

Combine milk, cream and vanilla in small pan, stir over low heat, bring slowly to boil, remove from heat, strain. Whisk eggs, sugar, cornflour and liqueur until slightly frothy and combined; pour warm milk over mixture, whisk until combined. Place cherries in pastry case, pour over egg mixture; bake in moderate oven about 45 minutes or until set. Serve immediately, sprinkled with extra sugar.

SERVES 6 TO 8

Pastry case can be made 3 days ahead.

Storage Airtight container
Freeze Uncooked pastry suitable
Microwave Not suitable

PINEAPPLE, COCONUT AND PALM SUGAR TARTLETS

1 quantity basic shortcrust pastry; recipe page 112

75g palm sugar

1¹/₂ tablespoons water

3 egg yolks

1 tablespoon cornflour

1 cup (250ml) coconut milk

¹/₄ cup (60ml) thickened cream, whipped

¹/₂ medium (600g) fresh pineapple, peeled, sliced

¹/₂ cup (25g) flaked coconut, toasted

GLAZE
50g palm sugar
2 tablespoons water

Grease 4 x 12cm round loose-base flan tins. Make pastry according to directions on page 112. Divide pastry into 4 portions. Roll each portion between sheets of baking paper until large enough to line prepared tins. Lift pastry into tins, ease into sides, trim edges. Lightly prick bases with fork, refrigerate 30 minutes.

Cover pastry with baking paper, fill with dried beans or rice, place on oven tray. Bake in moderately hot oven 10 minutes. Remove paper and beans carefully from pastry cases, bake further 15 minutes or until lightly browned; cool.

Combine sugar and water in small pan, stir over heat, without boiling, until sugar is dissolved, simmer, uncovered, without stirring, until mixture is light golden brown.

Combine egg yolks and cornflour in small bowl, beat with electric mixer until thick and creamy. Gradually add hot sugar syrup in a thin stream while motor is operating. Heat coconut milk in pan, stir in egg yolk mixture, stir over heat until mixture boils and thickens, poor mixture into bowl, cover; cool.

Fold in cream. Divide mixture between pastry cases, decorate with pineapple and coconut, brush pineapple with glaze.

Glaze Combine sugar and water in pan, stir over heat, without boiling, until sugar is dissolved. Simmer, uncovered, without stirring, until glaze is light golden brown.

MAKES 4

Pastry cases can be made 3 days ahead.

Storage Airtight container
Freeze Uncooked pastry suitable
Microwave Not suitable

Left, from top Warm berry compote; Apple hazelnut tart
Above, from top Cherry clafouti; Pineapple, coconut and palm sugar tartlets

ORANGE AND WHITE CHOCOLATE TARTLETS

We used blood oranges in this recipe, but any oranges are suitable.

2¹/₃ cups (350g) plain flour
²/₃ cup (150g) caster sugar
250g butter, melted
6 medium (1.8kg) oranges, segmented, seeded

FILLING
3 egg yolks
2 tablespoons caster sugar
¹/₄ cup (60ml) orange juice concentrate
¹/₄ cup (60ml) thickened cream
60g butter
120g white chocolate, finely grated
2 teaspoons Grand Marnier

SAUCE
1¹/₂ tablespoons sugar
2 teaspoons cornflour
1 cup (250ml) fresh orange juice
¹/₂ vanilla bean, split

Process flour and sugar until combined, add butter and pulse until ingredients just come together. Press dough into a ball, knead gently on lightly floured surface until smooth. Wrap in plastic, refrigerate 30 minutes.

Divide pastry into 6 portions, press each portion evenly over bases and sides of 6 deep 10cm round loose-base flan tins; trim edges. Place on oven tray, refrigerate 30 minutes. Bake in moderate oven about 20 minutes or until golden brown; cool.

Pour filling into pastry cases, cool 1 hour, refrigerate until firm. Place orange segments on filling, brush with a little of the sauce, serve tartlets with remaining sauce.

Filling Whisk egg yolks, sugar and juice in medium bowl until sugar is dissolved. Bring cream and butter to gentle boil in heavy-based pan. Gradually whisk hot cream mixture into egg mixture. Return custard to pan, whisk over low heat, without boiling, until thickened. Remove from heat, add chocolate and liqueur, whisk until smooth.

Sauce Blend sugar and cornflour with juice in pan, add vanilla bean, stir constantly over heat until mixture boils and thickens; strain.

MAKES 6

Recipe can be made a day ahead.

Storage Covered, separately, in refrigerator
Freeze Uncooked pastry and sauce suitable
Microwave Sauce suitable

PEAR AND ALMOND TART

3 medium (540g) firm pears, peeled, cored, halved
2 tablespoons lemon juice
¹/₄ cup (60ml) Armagnac or brandy
1¹/₂ cups (225g) plain flour
²/₃ cup (80g) packaged ground almonds
¹/₃ cup (75g) caster sugar
185g cold unsalted butter
2 egg yolks
³/₄ cup (180ml) thickened cream

ALMOND FILLING
125g soft butter
¹/₄ teaspoon almond essence
¹/₂ cup (110g) caster sugar
2 eggs
1 tablespoon plain flour
1 cup (125g) packaged ground almonds

Brush pears with juice, place in shallow ovenproof dish; sprinkle with 2 tablespoons of the brandy, cover, bake in moderate oven about 20 minutes or until just tender; cool. Strain pears, reserve liquid.

Sift flour into bowl, add nuts and sugar, rub in butter (or process flour, nuts, sugar and butter until mixture resembles breadcrumbs). Add egg yolks, mix until ingredients cling together (or process until ingredients just come together). Press dough into a ball, wrap in plastic, refrigerate 1 hour.

Roll two-thirds of the pastry between sheets of floured baking paper until large enough to line 3.5cm deep x 24cm round loose-base flan tin, ease into side, trim edge. Lightly prick base with fork, refrigerate 30 minutes.

Spread almond filling over base of pastry case, place pears around edge. Roll remaining pastry between sheets of floured baking paper until large enough to cover tart, cut 5cm circle from centre, gently cover pears with pastry, trim edge. Brush with water, sprinkle with a little extra sugar. Bake in moderate oven about 1 hour or until browned. Stand 15 minutes before serving. Dust with sifted icing sugar, if desired.

Beat cream until soft peaks form; fold in reserved liquid and remaining brandy, serve with tart.

Almond Filling Cream butter, essence and sugar in small bowl with electric mixer until thick and creamy, add eggs 1 at a time, beating well after each addition; fold in flour and nuts.

SERVES 6 TO 8

Pears can be cooked a day ahead.

Storage Covered, in refrigerator
Freeze Uncooked pastry suitable
Microwave Pears suitable

Left Pear and almond tart
Above Orange and white chocolate tartlets

STRAWBERRY FLAN

**1 quantity basic shortcrust pastry;
recipe page 112**
500g strawberries
**2 tablespoons raspberry jam,
warmed, sieved**

FILLING
300ml sour cream
**¼ cup (40g) icing sugar
mixture, sifted**
1 tablespoon Grand Marnier
1 teaspoon grated orange rind

Make pastry according to directions on
page 112. Roll pastry between sheets of
baking paper until large enough to line
11cm x 35cm rectangular loose-base flan
tin (or 20cm round loose-base flan tin).

Lift pastry into tin, ease into sides, trim
edges. Lightly prick base with fork,
refrigerate 30 minutes.

Cover pastry with baking paper, fill
with dried beans or rice, place on oven
tray. Bake in moderately hot oven
10 minutes. Remove paper and beans
carefully from pastry case, bake further
15 minutes or until lightly browned; cool.
Spread filling into pastry case, top evenly
with strawberries, brush with jam.

Filling Combine all ingredients in bowl;
mix well.

SERVES 6

Recipe can be made a day ahead.

Storage Covered, in refrigerator
Freeze Uncooked pastry suitable
Microwave Not suitable

CHOCOLATE BROWNIE TART

2 cups (300g) plain flour
½ cup (80g) icing sugar mixture
125g cold butter, chopped
1 egg yolk
1 teaspoon vanilla essence

FILLING
200g milk chocolate, chopped
200g dark chocolate, chopped
125g butter, chopped
4 egg yolks
1 egg, lightly beaten
¼ cup (55g) caster sugar
1 tablespoon Creme de Cacao

Grease 24cm round loose-base flan tin.
Sift flour and sugar into bowl, rub in
butter (or process flour, sugar and butter
until mixture resembles breadcrumbs).
Add egg yolk and essence, mix until all
ingredients cling together (or process
until all ingredients just come together).
Press dough into a ball, knead gently on
a lightly floured surface until smooth.
Cover dough with plastic wrap, refrigerate
30 minutes.

Roll pastry between sheets of floured
baking paper until large enough to line
prepared tin. Lift pastry into tin, ease
into side, trim edge. Lightly prick base
with form, refrigerate 30 minutes.

Cover pastry with baking paper, fill
with dried beans or rice, place on oven
tray. Bake in moderately hot oven
12 minutes. Remove paper and beans
carefully from pastry case, bake further
10 minutes or until lightly browned; cool.

Spoon filling into pastry case, bake in
moderately slow oven about 40 minutes
or until edge of tart is firm (the middle
will still look slightly unset). Stand
20 minutes before serving. Serve dusted
with sifted icing sugar and whipped
cream, if desired.

Filling Combine chocolate with butter in
heatproof bowl over pan of simmering
water, stir until smooth; cool 10 minutes.
Beat egg yolks, egg and sugar in small
bowl with electric mixer until thick and
creamy. Transfer to medium bowl,
gradually beat in chocolate mixture and
liqueur, beat until smooth.

SERVES 8

Recipe can be made a day ahead.

Storage Covered, in refrigerator
Freeze Suitable
Microwave Not suitable

Left Strawberry flan
Right, from top Chocolate brownie tart;
Apple sable

APPLE SABLE

4 medium (600g) apples, peeled
50g butter
2 tablespoons brown sugar
2 tablespoons dark rum

ALMOND PASTRY
1¹/₃ cups (200g) plain flour
¹/₄ cup (55g) caster sugar
¹/₂ cup (60g) packaged
  ground almonds
150g cold butter, chopped
2 egg yolks
1 tablespoon iced water,
  approximately

CREME ANGLAISE
1 cup (250ml) milk
1 vanilla bean, split
2 egg yolks
2 tablespoons caster sugar

Cut apples into quarters, cut each quarter into 4 slices. Heat butter in pan, add sugar, stir over heat, without boiling, until sugar is dissolved. Add apples, cook, stirring, until apples are lightly browned; stir in rum.

Place a pastry circle on each serving plate, top each pastry circle with quarter of the apple mixture, then remaining pastry circles; dust with sifted icing sugar, if desired. Serve with creme anglaise.

Almond Pastry Combine flour, sugar and nuts in processor bowl, add butter, process until mixture resembles breadcrumbs. Add egg yolks and enough water to make ingredients cling together. Press dough into a ball, knead gently on lightly floured surface until smooth. Wrap in plastic, refrigerate 30 minutes.

Roll pastry between sheets of baking paper until large enough to cut 8 x 9cm circles. Place circles on greased oven trays. Lightly prick pastry with fork, refrigerate 30 minutes. Bake pastry in moderately hot oven about 10 minutes or until lightly browned; cool.

Creme Anglaise Combine milk and vanilla bean in small pan, bring to boil, remove from heat, stand, covered, 15 minutes. Strain mixture through fine cloth. Beat egg yolks and sugar in small bowl with electric mixer until thick and creamy, gradually add milk. Return mixture to pan, stir over low heat, without boiling, about 10 minutes or until slightly thickened. Strain mixture, cover; cool. Refrigerate until cold.

SERVES 4

Almond pastry and creme anglaise can be made a day ahead.

Storage Pastry, in airtight container. Creme anglaise, covered, in refrigerator
Freeze Uncooked pastry suitable
Microwave Not suitable

GATEAU ST HONORE

**1 sheet ready-rolled
  shortcrust pastry**
1 egg yolk
**2 quantities basic choux pastry;
  recipe page 113**
500g strawberries
230g blueberries

FILLINGS
6 egg yolks
1/2 cup (110g) caster sugar
2 tablespoons plain flour
2 tablespoons cornflour
2 cups (500ml) milk
1 vanilla bean, split
1/4 cup (60ml) Cointreau
2 teaspoons grated orange rind
100g soft butter
1 cup (250ml) sour cream

TOFFEE
1 1/2 cups (330g) caster sugar
3/4 cup (180ml) water

Cut 24cm round from shortcrust pastry, place on greased oven tray, prick all over with fork, brush edge with egg yolk.

Make choux pastry according to directions on page 113. Drop 12 level tablespoons of choux pastry 5cm apart onto greased oven trays. Bake in hot oven 10 minutes, reduce heat to moderately hot, bake further 30 minutes or until browned and crisp. Cool on wire rack.

Using a metal spatula, spread 1 cup (250ml) of the choux pastry evenly over shortcrust pastry round. Then, using pastry bag fitted with 12mm plain tube, pipe rings of choux pastry just inside edge of round.

Bake in hot oven 15 minutes, reduce heat to moderately hot, bake further 40 minutes. Cut a slit in side of base to allow steam to escape. Return to oven about another 5 minutes or until browned and crisp. Cool on wire rack.

Using a skewer, make small holes in base of each small puff. Spoon liqueur filling into piping bag fitted with small plain tube, pipe filling into puffs. Fill centre of ring with the cream filling, top with berries.

Dip base of 1 puff quickly into toffee, place on edge of pastry ring. Repeat with remaining puffs. Spoon a little more toffee over puffs. Dip a fork into remaining toffee, and, using a flicking action, flick toffee over greased foil so that threads of toffee form a nest; carefully lift onto gateau.

Fillings Combine egg yolks, sugar, and sifted flours in bowl, whisk until smooth. Combine milk and vanilla bean in pan, bring to boil, remove vanilla bean. Gradually whisk hot milk into egg mixture, return mixture to pan, whisk constantly over heat until mixture boils and thickens; transfer to bowl. Stir in liqueur and rind, cover; cool.

Divide mixture in half. Beat half the filling with butter in small bowl of electric mixer until smooth and changed in colour; reserve liqueur filling to fill puffs. Fold cream into remaining mixture; reserve cream filling to fill ring.

Toffee Combine sugar and water in pan, stir over heat, without boiling, until sugar is dissolved. Bring to boil, boil, uncovered, without stirring, about 10 minutes or until mixture is golden brown. Remove from heat, stand pan in heatproof bowl of hot water to prevent toffee from setting.

SERVES 8

Choux base, puffs and fillings can be made a day ahead. Best assembled close to serving. Toffee must be made just before required.

Storage Base and puffs, in airtight container. Fillings, covered, in refrigerator
Freeze Unfilled cooked base and puffs suitable
Microwave Not suitable

CHOCOLATE COCONUT STRUDEL

40g soft butter
1/4 cup (55g) caster sugar
2 eggs, separated
100g dark chocolate, grated
1/3 cup (30g) coconut
1/3 cup (40g) packaged ground almonds
1 tablespoon caster sugar, extra
6 sheets fillo pastry
50g butter, melted, extra

COCONUT CREAM SAUCE
300ml cream
1/2 cup (125ml) coconut milk
1 vanilla bean, split
3 egg yolks
2 tablespoons caster sugar

Cream butter and sugar in small bowl with electric mixer until light and fluffy, beat in egg yolks 1 at a time, beat until combined. Transfer mixture to large bowl, stir in chocolate, coconut and nuts.

Beat egg whites and extra sugar in small bowl until firm peaks form, fold into chocolate mixture.

Layer pastry sheets together, brushing each with extra butter. Spoon chocolate mixture down 1 long edge of pastry, leaving 8cm border at each end. Roll up strudel, tucking in ends while rolling, brush with extra butter. Place strudel on lightly greased oven tray, bake in moderate oven about 30 minutes or until browned. Stand strudel 30 minutes before serving. Dust with sifted icing sugar, if desired. Serve with coconut cream sauce.

Coconut Cream Sauce Combine cream, coconut milk and vanilla bean in small pan, bring to boil, remove from heat, stand, covered, 15 minutes; strain.

Beat egg yolks and sugar in small bowl with electric mixer until thick and creamy, gradually beat in cream mixture. Return mixture to pan, stir over low heat, without boiling, until slightly thickened. Strain mixture, cover; cool. Refrigerate 3 hours or overnight.

SERVES 6

Strudel can be prepared a day ahead. Sauce can be made a day ahead.

Storage Covered, separately, in refrigerator
Freeze Not suitable
Microwave Not suitable

APPLE AND GINGER TARTLETS

1 quantity basic pate sucree; recipe page 113
2 small (260g) apples, cored, thinly sliced
60g butter, chopped
1 tablespoon caster sugar
2 tablespoons plum jam
2 teaspoons green ginger wine

APPLE PUREE
2 medium (300g) apples, peeled, cored, chopped
1/2 teaspoon grated lemon rind
1 tablespoon caster sugar
2 tablespoons water
1/4 cup (50g) chopped glace ginger

Make pastry according to directions on page 113. Divide pastry into 4 portions. Roll each portion between sheets of floured baking paper to 15cm circle, turn in 5mm border, pinch edges to decorate. Place on greased oven trays, refrigerate 30 minutes.

Spread apple puree over pastry, top with apples, dot with butter, sprinkle with sugar. Bake in moderately hot oven about 20 minutes or until apples are tender. Brush hot tarts with combined warmed jam and wine.

Apple Puree Combine apples, rind, sugar and water in pan, simmer, covered, about 10 minutes or until apples are pulpy. Stir until smooth, add ginger; cool.

MAKES 4

Pastry bases can be made 3 days ahead. Apple puree can be made a day ahead.

Storage Pastry, in airtight container. Apple puree, covered, in refrigerator
Freeze Uncooked pastry suitable
Microwave Apple puree suitable

Right Chocolate coconut strudel
Far right, from top Apple and ginger tartlets; Macadamia chocolate tartlets

MACADAMIA CHOCOLATE TARTLETS

1¹/4 cups (185g) plain flour
1 tablespoon caster sugar
¹/2 cup (45g) coconut
125g cold butter, chopped
1 egg, lightly beaten, approximately
50g dark chocolate, chopped
125g unsalted macadamias,
  coarsely chopped
2 eggs, lightly beaten, extra
¹/2 cup (125ml) light corn syrup
¹/3 cup (65g) firmly packed
  brown sugar
30g butter, melted, extra

Combine flour, sugar and coconut in processor bowl, add butter, process until mixture resembles breadcrumbs. Add enough egg to make ingredients cling together. Press dough into a ball, knead on floured surface until smooth. Wrap in plastic, refrigerate 30 minutes.

Divide pastry into 4 portions, roll each portion between sheets of baking paper until large enough to line 4 x 3cm-deep x 10cm round loose-base flan tins. Lift pastry into tins, ease into sides, trim edges. Lightly prick bases with fork, refrigerate 30 minutes.

Cover pastry with baking paper, fill with dried beans or rice, place on oven tray. Bake in moderately hot oven 10 minutes. Remove paper and beans carefully from pastry cases, bake further 10 minutes or until lightly browned; cool.

Divide chocolate and nuts between pastry cases, pour over combined extra eggs, corn syrup, brown sugar and melted extra butter. Bake in moderate oven 15 minutes, reduce temperature to moderately slow, bake further 20 minutes or until filling is set.

MAKES 4

Pastry cases can be made 3 days ahead.

Storage Airtight container
Freeze Uncooked pastry suitable
Microwave Not suitable

ROSE PETAL TARTLETS

Be sure to use rose petals which have not been treated with insecticides or pesticides.

1 quantity basic biscuit pastry; recipe page 113
1 egg, lightly beaten
1 tablespoon caster sugar
1/3 cup (80ml) milk
1/3 cup (80ml) thickened cream
3 teaspoons rosewater
6 fresh rose petals

FROSTED ROSE PETALS
18 fresh rose petals
1 egg white, lightly beaten
1/2 cup (110g) caster sugar

Make pastry according to directions on page 113. Divide pastry into 6 portions, roll each portion between sheets of floured baking paper until large enough to line 6 x 9.5cm brioche tins (100ml capacity). Lift pastry into tins, ease into sides, trim edges. Lightly prick bases with fork, refrigerate 30 minutes.

Cover pastry with baking paper, fill with dried beans or rice; place on oven tray. Bake in moderately hot oven 10 minutes. Remove paper and beans carefully from pastry cases, bake further 10 minutes or until browned; cool.

Combine egg with sugar in bowl, stir in milk, cream and rosewater. Place a rose petal in each pastry case, fill with cream mixture. Bake in moderately hot oven 15 minutes, cover with foil, bake further 5 minutes or until custard is set; cool. Dust with sifted icing sugar, if desired; top with frosted rose petals.

Frosted Rose Petals Brush petals very lightly all over with egg white. Sprinkle lightly with sugar; stand on wire rack about 1 hour or until dry.

MAKES 6

Tartlets and frosted rose petals can be made a day ahead.

Storage Separately, in airtight containers
Freeze Uncooked pastry suitable
Microwave Not suitable

ICE CREAM PIE WITH CHOCOLATE BRANDY SAUCE

1¹/₂ cups (225g) plain flour
1/4 cup (40g) icing sugar mixture
1 tablespoon cocoa
125g cold butter, chopped
1 egg yolk
3 teaspoons iced water, approximately
1 litre (4 cups) vanilla ice-cream
1 litre (4 cups) chocolate ice-cream

CHOCOLATE BRANDY SAUCE
200g milk chocolate, melted
1 tablespoon brandy
2/3 cup (160ml) thickened cream

Sift flour, sugar and cocoa into bowl, rub in butter (or process flour, sugar, cocoa and butter until mixture resembles breadcrumbs). Add egg yolk and enough water to make ingredients cling together (or process until ingredients just come together). Press dough into a ball, knead gently on floured surface until smooth. Wrap in plastic, refrigerate 30 minutes.

Roll pastry between sheets of baking paper until large enough to line 24cm round loose-base flan tin. Lift pastry into tin, ease into side, trim edge. Lightly prick base with fork, refrigerate 30 minutes.

Cover pastry with baking paper, fill with dried beans or rice, place on oven tray. Bake in moderately hot oven 10 minutes. Remove paper and beans carefully from pastry case, bake further 10 minutes; cool.

Fill pastry case with scoops of vanilla and chocolate ice-creams, serve with chocolate brandy sauce.

Chocolate Brandy Sauce Combine all ingredients in bowl; stir until smooth.

SERVES 8

Pastry case and sauce can be made a day ahead.

Storage Covered, separately, in refrigerator
Freeze Uncooked pastry suitable
Microwave Not suitable

PEACH AND PECAN PIE

1 quantity basic pate sucree; recipe page 113

FILLING
4 medium (800g) peaches
1/2 cup (125ml) thickened cream
3 eggs
1/3 cup (75g) caster sugar
1/3 cup (35g) pecans, finely chopped

Make pastry according to directions on page 113. Roll pastry between sheets of floured baking paper until large enough to line 24cm round loose-base flan tin. Lift pastry into tin, ease into side, trim edge. Lightly prick base with fork, refrigerate 30 minutes.

Cover pastry with baking paper, fill with dried beans or rice, place on oven tray. Bake in moderately hot oven 10 minutes. Remove paper and beans carefully from pastry case, bake further 10 minutes or until lightly browned; cool. Pour filling into pastry case, bake in moderately slow oven about 40 minutes or until just set; dust with sifted icing sugar, if desired.

Filling Peel and chop peaches; discard seeds. Combine peaches and cream in pan, simmer, covered, 5 minutes or until peaches are soft; cover, cool until mixture is warm. Whisk eggs and sugar in bowl until combined, stir in peach mixture and nuts; mix well.

SERVES 6

Recipe can be made a day ahead.

Storage Covered, in refrigerator
Freeze Uncooked pastry suitable
Microwave Not suitable

Left Rose petal tartlets
Above Ice cream pie with chocolate brandy sauce
Right Peach and pecan pie

FRESH DATE TARTS

1 quantity basic biscuit pastry;
    recipe page 113
60g butter
1/2 cup (125ml) golden syrup
1/2 cup (125ml) coconut cream
1/4 teaspoon ground cardamom
1/4 teaspoon ground cinnamon
24 large (500g) fresh dates, halved

SPICED CREAM
300ml thickened cream
1/2 teaspoon ground cinnamon
1/2 teaspoon ground nutmeg
1/2 teaspoon vanilla essence

Make pastry according to directions on page 113. Divide pastry into 6 portions. Roll each portion between sheets of floured baking paper until large enough to line 6 deep 10cm round loose-base flan tins. Lift pastry into tins, ease into sides, trim edges. Lightly prick bases with fork, refrigerate 30 minutes.

Cover pastry with baking paper, fill with dried beans or rice, place tins on oven tray. Bake in moderately hot oven 10 minutes. Remove paper and beans carefully from pastry cases, bake further 10 minutes or until browned; cool.

Combine butter, syrup, cream and spices in pan, stir over low heat until mixture is bubbling. Add dates, stir gently, remove dates; cool. Simmer mixture 15 minutes or until reduced to 3/4 cup (180ml).

Pour a little of the butter mixture into pastry cases, top with dates, carefully pour remaining butter mixture over dates. Return tarts to moderate oven 5 minutes so caramel melts evenly. Cool to room temperature, serve with spiced cream.

Spiced Cream Beat all ingredients in small bowl until soft peaks form.

MAKES 6

Pastry cases can be made 3 days ahead.

Storage Airtight container
Freeze Uncooked pastry suitable
Microwave Not suitable

CUSTARD TART

1 quantity basic biscuit pastry;
    recipe page 113
3 eggs, lightly beaten
1 teaspoon vanilla essence
1/4 cup (55g) caster sugar
2 cups (500ml) hot milk
ground nutmeg

Grease 23cm pie plate. Make pastry according to directions on page 113. Roll pastry between sheets of floured baking paper until large enough to line prepared plate. Lift pastry into plate, ease into side, trim edge. Cut scraps into strips to make a double layer of pastry around edge of plate, join pastry with a little water. Trim edge, pinch edge to decorate; refrigerate 30 minutes.

Cover pastry with baking paper, fill with dried beans or rice, place on oven tray. Bake in moderately hot oven 10 minutes. Remove paper and beans carefully from pastry case, bake further 10 minutes or until lightly browned; cool.

Whisk eggs, essence and sugar in bowl until combined. Quickly whisk hot milk into egg mixture. Pour custard slowly into pastry case, bake in moderate oven 15 minutes. Sprinkle custard with nutmeg, bake further 15 minutes or until custard is just set; cool.

SERVES 6 TO 8

Recipe can be made a day ahead.

Storage Covered, in refrigerator
Freeze Uncooked pastry suitable
Microwave Not suitable

PEACH AND BLUEBERRY COBBLER

15 small (1.7kg) slipstone peaches
250g blueberries
1/4 cup (55g) caster sugar

PASTRY
21/2 cups (375g) self-raising flour
1 teaspoon ground cinnamon
1/4 teaspoon ground nutmeg
1/4 cup (55g) caster sugar
1 teaspoon grated orange rind
90g cold butter, chopped
3/4 cup (180ml) cream
1 tablespoon iced water,
    approximately

Add peaches in batches to pan of boiling water for 30 seconds, remove with slotted spoon, immediately transfer to bowl of iced water. Drain peaches, peel and quarter. Combine peaches, blueberries and sugar in bowl, spoon into shallow ovenproof dish (2 litre/8 cup capacity), top with pastry shapes. Bake in moderately hot oven about 40 minutes or until golden brown.

Pastry Sift flour and spices into bowl, stir in sugar and rind, rub in butter (or process flour, spices, sugar, rind and butter until mixture resembles fine breadcrumbs). Add cream and enough water to make ingredients cling together (or process until mixture just comes together). Do not over-mix. Roll pastry on lightly floured surface until 1cm thick, cut into enough shapes to cover fruit.

SERVES 6

Recipe best made close to serving.

Freeze Uncooked pastry suitable
Microwave Not suitable

Above Fresh date tarts
Right, from top Custard tart; Peach and blueberry cobbler

PEAR TARTS WITH ORANGE LIQUEUR SAUCE

2 medium (360g) firm pears
1 sheet ready-rolled puff pastry
1 egg, lightly beaten

GLAZE
¼ cup (60ml) apricot jam
½ teaspoon gelatine
1 tablespoon water
1 tablespoon Grand Marnier

ORANGE LIQUEUR SAUCE
2 tablespoons caster sugar
2 egg yolks
1 cup (250ml) cream
3 teaspoons Grand Marnier
1 teaspoon grated orange rind

Peel and core pears, leaving stems intact. Cut pears and stems in half. Using a canelle knife, cut grooves into pear halves at an angle.

Cut pastry into quarters, top each quarter with half a pear. Trim pastry to the shape of the pear, leaving 1.5cm border around pear. Place on greased oven tray; brush pastry with egg. Bake in very hot oven 15 minutes, reduce heat to moderately hot, bake about 20 minutes or until pears are tender. Brush hot tarts with glaze; cool to room temperature. Serve with orange liqueur sauce.

Glaze Combine all ingredients in small pan, stir over heat until warm; strain.

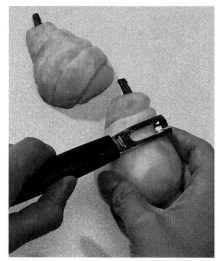

Orange Liqueur Sauce Whisk sugar and egg yolks in small pan until creamy; stir in cream. Stir over low heat, without boiling, until mixture coats back of metal spoon. Stir in liqueur and rind; cool.

MAKES 4

Tarts and sauce can be made a day ahead.

Storage Covered, in refrigerator
Freeze Cooked tarts suitable
Microwave Not suitable

MANDARIN AND CARDAMOM TARTLETS

1¼ cups (185g) plain flour
¼ cup (40g) icing sugar mixture
½ cup (60g) packaged
 ground almonds
125g cold butter, chopped
1 egg, lightly beaten
3 medium (250g) mandarins,
 segmented, seeded
⅓ cup (80ml) orange
 marmalade, warmed

FILLING
3 egg yolks
¼ cup (55g) caster sugar
1½ tablespoons plain flour
1 cup (250ml) milk
50g soft butter
⅓ cup (55g) icing sugar mixture
⅓ cup (40g) packaged
 ground almonds
1 egg yolk, extra

CARDAMOM CREAM
½ teaspoon ground cardamom
2 tablespoons sour cream

Grease 6 x 9.5cm brioche tins (100ml capacity). Sift flour and sugar into bowl, stir in nuts, rub in butter (or process flour, sugar, nuts and butter until mixture resembles breadcrumbs). Add egg, mix until ingredients cling together (or process until ingredients just come together). Press dough into a ball, knead gently on lightly floured surface until smooth. Wrap in plastic, refrigerate 30 minutes.

Divide pastry into 6 portions. Roll each portion between sheets of baking paper until large enough to line prepared tins. Lift pastry into tins, press into sides, trim edges. Place tins on oven tray; refrigerate 30 minutes.

Divide filling between pastry cases, bake in moderately hot oven about 25 minutes or until browned; cool in tins. Just before serving, spread with cardamom cream, top with mandarin segments, brush with sieved marmalade.

Filling Combine egg yolks, sugar and flour in bowl, whisk until smooth. Bring milk just to the boil in pan, remove from heat, gradually whisk into egg mixture. Return mixture to heat, whisk constantly until mixture boils and thickens. Remove from heat, continue to whisk until smooth; cover, cool. Divide mixture into 2 portions, reserve 1 portion for cardamom cream.

Beat butter and sifted icing sugar in small bowl with electric mixer until combined, beat in nuts, extra egg yolk and half the filling mixture.

Cardamom Cream Combine reserved filling mixture with cardamom and sour cream in small bowl; mix well.

MAKES 6

Pastry, filling and cardamom cream can be made a day ahead. Pastry can be cooked with filling a day ahead.

Storage Pastry, in airtight container. Filling and cardamom cream, covered, in refrigerator. Cooked pastry with filling, covered, in refrigerator
Freeze Uncooked pastry suitable
Microwave Not suitable

Left Pear tarts with orange liqueur sauce
Below Mandarin and cardamom tartlets

GRAPE FLAN WITH LIQUEUR CREAM CHEESE FILLING

1 quantity basic pate sucree; recipe page 113
500g seedless white grapes

FILLING
250g cream cheese
1/2 cup (125ml) sour cream
1/2 cup (80g) icing sugar mixture
2 tablespoons orange juice
1 tablespoon Grand Marnier
2 teaspoons gelatine
1 tablespoon water

GLAZE
1/3 cup (80ml) apricot jam
1 teaspoon cornflour
2 tablespoons water

Make pastry according to directions on page 113. Roll pastry between sheets of floured baking paper until large enough to line 11cm x 35cm rectangular or 20cm round loose-base flan tin. Lift pastry into tin, ease into side, trim edge. Lightly prick base with fork, refrigerate 30 minutes.

Cover pastry with baking paper, fill with dried beans or rice, place on oven tray. Bake in moderately hot oven 10 minutes. Remove paper and beans carefully from pastry case. Bake further 10 minutes or until browned; cool.

Spoon filling into pastry case, refrigerate 30 minutes. Place grapes over filling, brush with glaze, refrigerate.

Filling Beat cheese and sour cream in small bowl until smooth; gradually beat in sifted icing sugar, juice and liqueur. Sprinkle gelatine over water in cup, stand in small pan of simmering water, stir until dissolved; stir into cheese mixture.

Glaze Sieve jam into pan, stir in blended cornflour and water, stir over heat until mixture boils and thickens slightly. Cool 10 minutes before using.

SERVES 6

Recipe can be made a day ahead.

Storage Covered, in refrigerator
Freeze Uncooked pastry suitable
Microwave Gelatine and glaze suitable

RASPBERRY LINZER TORTE

1 2/3 cups (250g) plain flour
2/3 cup (110g) pure icing sugar
2 tablespoons cocoa
1/4 teaspoon ground cloves
2 teaspoons ground cinnamon
3/4 cup (90g) packaged ground almonds
1 teaspoon grated lemon rind
125g cold butter, chopped
1 teaspoon vanilla essence
1 egg, lightly beaten

ALMOND CREAM
100g soft butter
2/3 cup (110g) pure icing sugar
2 eggs, lightly beaten
3/4 cup (90g) packaged ground almonds

RASPBERRY TOPPING
1 cup (250ml) raspberry jam
350g fresh raspberries

Sift flour, sugar, cocoa and spices into bowl, stir in nuts and rind; rub in butter (or process flour, sugar, cocoa, spices, nuts, rind and butter until mixture resembles breadcrumbs). Add essence and egg to make ingredients cling together (or process until ingredients just come together). Press dough into a ball, knead on floured surface until smooth. Wrap in plastic, refrigerate 30 minutes.

Roll two-thirds of the pastry between sheets of baking paper until large enough to line 3.5cm deep x 24cm loose-base flan tin. Lift pastry into tin, ease into side, trim edge. Spread almond cream into pastry case, refrigerate 30 minutes.

Top almond cream with raspberry topping. Roll out remaining pastry, cut into strips, place strips across raspberry mixture to create a lattice effect. Place torte on oven tray, bake in moderate oven about 55 minutes or until browned. Sift icing sugar over hot torte. Refrigerate until cold.

Almond Cream Beat butter and sugar in small bowl with electric mixer until pale and creamy. Beat in eggs 1 at a time; stir in nuts.

Raspberry Topping Process jam and berries until combined; strain.

SERVES 6 TO 8

Recipe can be made a day ahead.

Storage Covered, in refrigerator
Freeze Uncooked pastry suitable
Microwave Not suitable

Left Grape flan with liqueur cream cheese filling
Right Raspberry linzer torte

APRICOT BAKEWELL TART

1 quantity basic biscuit pastry;
    recipe page 113
2 tablespoons apricot jam
825g can apricot halves, drained
100g soft butter
$^1/_2$ cup (110g) caster sugar
2 eggs
$^1/_4$ cup (35g) self-raising flour
$^1/_2$ cup (60g) packaged
    ground almonds
1 teaspoon grated lemon rind
pinch ground cinnamon
2 tablespoons milk
$^1/_3$ cup (25g) flaked almonds

Make pastry according to directions on
page 113. Roll pastry between sheets of
floured baking paper until large enough
to line 24cm round loose-base flan tin.
Lift pastry into tin, ease into side, trim
edge. Lightly prick pastry with fork,
refrigerate 30 minutes. Spread jam over
pastry base. Pat apricots dry with
absorbent paper; place cut side down
over jam.

Cream butter and sugar in small bowl
with electric mixer until light and fluffy;
beat in eggs 1 at a time. Fold in sifted
flour, ground almonds, rind, cinnamon
and milk.

Top apricots with butter mixture,
sprinkle with flaked almonds. Bake in hot
oven 20 minutes, cover with foil, reduce
heat to moderate. Bake further 1 hour or
until firm.

SERVES 6

Recipe can be made a day ahead.

Storage Covered, in refrigerator
Freeze Uncooked pastry suitable
Microwave Not suitable

RASPBERRY ORANGE
MASCARPONE TART

1$^1/_2$ cups (225g) plain flour
1 tablespoon caster sugar
125g cold butter, chopped
1 teaspoon finely grated
    orange rind
2 tablespoons orange juice,
    approximately
400g fresh raspberries

FILLING

250g mascarpone cheese
$^1/_2$ cup (125ml) thickened cream
1 tablespoon Grand Marnier
1 tablespoon icing sugar mixture

GLAZE

$^1/_2$ cup (125ml) raspberry jam
1 tablespoon water

Sift flour and sugar into bowl, rub in
butter and rind (or process these
ingredients until mixture resembles
breadcrumbs). Add enough juice to make
ingredients cling together (or process
until ingredients just come together).
Press dough into a ball, knead on floured
surface until smooth. Wrap in plastic,
refrigerate 30 minutes.

Roll pastry between sheets of baking
paper until large enough to line 24cm
round loose-base flan tin. Lift pastry into
tin, ease into side, trim edge. Lightly
prick base with fork, refrigerate
30 minutes.

Cover pastry with baking paper, fill
with dried beans or rice, place on oven
tray. Bake in moderately hot oven
10 minutes. Remove paper and beans
carefully from pastry case, bake further
15 minutes or until browned; cool. Spread
filling into pastry case, top with

raspberries, brush with glaze.

Filling Combine all ingredients in small
bowl, beat with electric mixer or rotary
beater until soft peaks form.

Glaze Heat jam and water in small pan
until jam is melted; strain, discard seeds.

SERVES 6 TO 8

Recipe can be made a day ahead.

Storage Covered, in refrigerator
Freeze Uncooked pastry suitable
Microwave Glaze suitable

Left Apricot bakewell tart
Above Raspberry orange marscarpone tart

Mini sweet treats

Tiny, crisp pastries with irresistible fillings such as liqueur-laced creams and custards, fruit, chocolate, caramel and more are bite-sized brilliance. So delicious with after-dinner coffee or afternoon tea. Classic sweets such as neenish tarts, mini chocolate eclairs, baklava cigars and mini danish tarts are just some of the mini sweet treats that may be small in size but have huge appeal.

CHOCOLATE SURPRISE TARTLETS

Any flavoured liqueurs can be used in this recipe.

1 quantity basic pate sucree; recipe page 113
1/2 cup (75g) Choc Melts
10g butter
12 pistachios, toasted
12 hazelnuts, toasted

LIQUEUR FILLINGS
400g White Melts, chopped
300ml thickened cream
1 tablespoon Drambuie
1 tablespoon Frangelico

CHOCOLATE DECORATIONS
1/3 cup (60g) Choc Melts, melted

Grease 2 x 12-hole tartlet trays. Make pastry according to directions on page 113. Roll pastry between sheets of lightly floured baking paper until 2mm thick. Cut 24 x 7cm rounds, place in prepared trays, prick bases with fork; cover, refrigerate 30 minutes. Bake in moderately hot oven about 10 minutes or until lightly browned; cool.

Combine Choc Melts with butter in small heatproof bowl, stir over pan of simmering water until mixture is smooth. Using a pastry brush, brush inside surface of tartlet cases with the chocolate mixture. Allow tartlet cases to set at room temperature.

Place a nut in each tartlet case. Spoon Drambuie filling into piping bag fitted with small star tube, pipe filling over pistachios; top with a chocolate decoration. Repeat with Frangelico filling, piping over hazelnuts.

Liqueur Fillings Combine White Melts and cream in heatproof bowl, stir over pan of simmering water until mixture is smooth. Divide mixture into 2 portions, stir Drambuie into 1 portion and Frangelico into the other. Refrigerate until just thick. Beat each portion with electric mixer until just fluffy, about 30 seconds; do not over-beat.

Chocolate Decorations see page 114.

MAKES 24

Pastry cases can be made and brushed with chocolate a day ahead. Chocolate decorations can be made a day ahead.

Storage Separately, in airtight containers
Freeze Uncooked pastry suitable
Microwave Filling suitable

BABY TARTLETS WITH FRUIT

1½ cups (225g) plain flour
125g cold butter, chopped
1 egg yolk
3 teaspoons iced water, approximately
1 cup (250ml) creme fraiche
1 tablespoon icing sugar mixture

Sift flour into bowl, rub in butter (or process flour and butter until mixture resembles breadcrumbs). Add egg yolk and enough water to make ingredients cling together (or process until ingredients just come together). Press dough into a ball, knead gently on lightly floured surface until smooth. Wrap in plastic, refrigerate 30 minutes.

Divide pastry in half. Roll each half between sheets of baking paper until 3mm thick, cut into 4.5cm rounds. Place rounds into 4 x 12-hole (2 teaspoon capacity) tiny tartlet tins.

Prick bases of pastry with fork, bake in moderately hot oven 25 minutes or until lightly browned; cool. Top pastry cases with 1 teaspoon of combined creme fraiche and icing sugar. Decorate with fruit, as desired; dust with a little extra sifted icing sugar.

MAKES 48

Pastry cases can be made 3 days ahead.

Storage Airtight container
Freeze Uncooked pastry suitable
Microwave Not suitable

MINI CHOCOLATE ECLAIRS

½ quantity basic choux pastry; recipe page 113
¾ cup (180ml) thickened cream
1½ tablespoons icing sugar mixture
2 teaspoons Kahlua

TOPPING
100g dark chocolate, melted
2 teaspoons vegetable oil

Make pastry according to directions on page 113. Spoon mixture into piping bag fitted with 1cm plain tube, pipe 7cm lengths about 3cm apart onto greased oven trays, cut ends neatly with a wet knife. Bake in hot oven 10 minutes, reduce heat to moderately hot, bake further 15 minutes or until browned and crisp. Split eclairs in half, return to moderately hot oven further 5 minutes or until centres are dried out; cool.

Dip tops of eclairs in topping, refrigerate until set. Beat cream, sifted icing sugar and liqueur in small bowl until firm peaks form. Pipe cream mixture into bases of eclairs; replace tops.

Topping Combine chocolate and oil in small bowl; mix well.

MAKES ABOUT 40

Unfilled, uniced eclairs can be made a week ahead.

Storage Airtight container
Freeze Unfilled, uniced eclairs suitable
Microwave Topping suitable

NEENISH TARTS

1½ cups (225g) plain flour
100g cold butter
1 egg yolk
1 tablespoon lemon juice
1 tablespoon iced water

MOCK CREAM
⅓ cup (80ml) water
½ cup (110g) caster sugar
125g soft butter
1 teaspoon vanilla essence

GLACE ICING
1½ cups (240g) icing sugar mixture
2 tablespoons milk
½ teaspoon vanilla essence
1½ tablespoons cocoa
1½ teaspoons milk, extra

Grease 2 x 12-hole tartlet trays. Sift flour into bowl, rub in butter (or process flour and butter until mixture resembles breadcrumbs). Add egg yolk, juice and enough water to make ingredients cling together (or process until ingredients just come together). Press dough into a ball, knead gently on lightly floured surface

until smooth. Wrap in plastic, refrigerate 30 minutes.

Roll pastry on lightly floured surface until 2mm thick, cut into 7.5cm rounds. Line prepared trays with pastry rounds, prick pastry all over with fork, refrigerate 30 minutes. Bake in moderate oven about 12 minutes or until lightly browned. Lift pastry cases onto wire racks to cool.

Fill pastry cases with mock cream, level with spatula. Spread a teaspoon of vanilla icing over half of each tart, allow to set. Cover remaining half of each tart with chocolate icing.

Mock Cream Combine water and sugar in pan, stir over heat, without boiling, until sugar is dissolved. Bring to boil, remove from heat, cool to room temperature. Beat butter and essence in small bowl with electric mixer until as white as possible, gradually beat in cooled syrup; beat until light and fluffy.

Glace Icing Sift icing sugar into small bowl, stir in milk and essence, beat until smooth; divide mixture into 2 heatproof bowls. Stir sifted cocoa and extra milk into 1 bowl. Stir both icings separately over hot water until smooth.

MAKES 24

Recipe can be made 2 days ahead.

Storage Covered, in refrigerator
Freeze Uncooked pastry suitable
Microwave Not suitable

Left Baby tartlets with fruit
Above Mini chocolate eclairs
Right Neenish tarts

BAKLAVA CIGARS

1 cup (100g) walnuts,
  finely chopped
1 cup (150g) unroasted cashews,
  finely chopped
1/4 cup (55g) caster sugar
1 teaspoon dry instant coffee
1 teaspoon ground cinnamon
7 sheets fillo pastry
80g butter, melted

SYRUP
1 medium (140g) lemon
1/2 cup (110g) caster sugar
1 cup (250ml) water
1/4 cup (60ml) honey
1 cinnamon stick

Combine nuts, sugar, coffee and cinnamon in bowl. Cut 1 sheet of pastry crossways into 4 even strips, brush each strip with butter. Spoon 3 level teaspoons of nut mixture along end of each strip, leaving 3.5cm border. Fold in sides, brush with butter, roll up tightly to form a cigar shape. Repeat with remaining pastry, butter and nut mixture.

Place cigars onto greased oven trays, bake in moderately hot oven about 10 minutes or until lightly browned; cool on trays. Then place cigars in single layer in shallow dish, pour over warm syrup; cool.

Syrup Using vegetable peeler, peel rind thinly from half the lemon. Combine sugar with water in pan, stir over heat, without boiling, until sugar is dissolved. Add rind, honey and cinnamon to pan, simmer, uncovered, without stirring, 2 minutes; cool 10 minutes; strain.

MAKES 28

Cigars, without syrup, can be made a week ahead.

Storage Airtight container
Freeze Uncooked cigars suitable
Microwave Not suitable

CARAMEL BABY PALMIERS

2/3 cup (160ml) sweetened
  condensed milk
1/3 cup (65g) firmly packed
  brown sugar
1/3 cup (35g) ground hazelnuts
1/3 cup (40g) ground pecans
375g packet puff pastry
1 tablespoon caster sugar

Combine milk and brown sugar in pan, cook, stirring, until sugar is dissolved and mixture is light caramel colour. Add nuts; cool 20 minutes. Divide pastry in half. Roll 1 half on lightly floured surface to 19cm x 30cm rectangle, spread half the caramel mixture over rectangle.

Fold in long sides of rectangle so they meet in the centre, brush edges with water, fold in half lengthways, press lightly. Repeat with remaining pastry and caramel mixture. Cover rolls, refrigerate 30 minutes. Sprinkle rolls with caster sugar. Cut each roll into 1.5cm slices, place about 8cm apart on greased oven trays.

Preheat oven to highest temperature, place palmiers in oven, reduce temperature to moderately hot. Bake 10 minutes, turn palmiers with eggslice, bake about further 10 minutes or until crisp. Lift onto wire racks to cool. Lightly dust with sifted icing sugar, if desired.

MAKES ABOUT 30

Recipe can be made 2 days ahead.

Storage Airtight container
Freeze Uncooked palmiers suitable
Microwave Not suitable

From left Baklava cigars; Caramel baby palmiers

Spread butter to 13cm x 20cm rectangle onto foil. Refrigerate until ready to use.

Combine yeast, sugar and milk in bowl, cover, stand in warm place about 10 minutes or until frothy.

Sift flour into bowl, rub in extra butter, stir in extra sugar, egg and yeast mixture; mix to a firm dough. Knead dough on floured surface about 5 minutes or until smooth and elastic. Place dough in lightly oiled bowl, cover, stand in warm place about 1½ hours or until dough is doubled in size.

MINI DANISH PASTRIES

220g unsalted butter
2 teaspoons (7g) dried yeast
1 teaspoon sugar
½ cup (125ml) warm milk
2⅓ cups (350g) plain flour
30g unsalted butter, extra
¼ cup (55g) sugar, extra
1 egg, lightly beaten
¼ cup (60ml) plum jam

CUSTARD
2 tablespoons sugar
1 tablespoon cornflour
3 teaspoons plain flour
1 cup (250ml) milk
2 egg yolks
1½ tablespoons Cassis

GLAZE
1 egg yolk
3 teaspoons Cassis

ICING
**1½ cups (240g) icing
   sugar mixture**
2 tablespoons milk, approximately

Turn dough onto floured surface, knead until smooth. Roll dough to 25cm x 30cm rectangle, keep corners as square as possible. Peel foil away from butter, place butter in centre of dough. Fold short sides of dough over butter to join in centre.

Turn dough a quarter of a turn. Roll to 25cm x 46cm rectangle. Fold one third onto centre third, fold remaining third on top. Wrap in plastic, refrigerate 30 minutes or until butter is firm. Roll and fold twice more as before, refrigerating dough between rollings.

Cut dough in half; refrigerate half. Roll remaining dough to 25cm x 32cm rectangle, trim to 24cm x 30cm rectangle,

cut into 6cm squares. Place 1 level teaspoon custard in centre of each square, top with 1/4 teaspoon jam, brush edges lightly with glaze. Bring opposite corners together; pinch gently.

Cover oven trays with baking paper, place pastries on trays, stand in warm place about 20 minutes or until slightly risen. Repeat with remaining pastry, custard and jam.

Brush pastries lightly with glaze, bake in moderately hot oven about 12 minutes or until lightly browned. Drizzle warm pastries with warm icing.

Custard Combine sugar and flours in pan, gradually whisk in milk and egg yolks, cook, stirring, until mixture boils and thickens. Remove from heat, stir in liqueur. Cover surface with plastic wrap; cool. Refrigerate until cold.

Glaze Whisk egg yolk and liqueur together in bowl.

Icing Sift icing sugar into heatproof bowl, add enough milk to form a firm paste; tint with food colouring, if desired. Place bowl over pan of simmering water, stir until icing is pourable.

MAKES 40

Recipe can be made 2 days ahead.

Storage Covered, in refrigerator
Freeze Suitable
Microwave Not suitable

Left Mini danish pastries
Above Mini cream horns

MINI CREAM HORNS

Cream horn tins can be bought from kitchenware stores, usually in sets of 6. Cook 6 pastry cones at a time.

375g packet frozen puff pastry
milk
1/3 cup (80ml) jam

CHANTILLY CREAM
2 teaspoons icing sugar mixture
1/2 teaspoon vanilla essence
2/3 cup (160ml) thickened cream

Grease cream horn tins. Roll pastry on floured surface to 36cm x 60cm rectangle, cut into 30 x 2cm strips. Moisten 1 edge of each strip with water. Starting at point of tin, wind strips around tin, overlapping the moistened edge; do not stretch pastry. Bring pastry about 6cm up length of tin. Repeat with remaining pastry.

Place tins about 3cm apart on greased oven tray, brush pastry lightly and evenly with milk. Bake in hot oven 10 minutes, slip cones off tins, reduce to moderate, bake further 15 minutes or until crisp. Cool on wire rack. Spoon a little jam into cones, pipe in Chantilly cream just before serving. Dust with sifted icing sugar, if desired.

Chantilly Cream Combine all ingredients in bowl, refrigerate 30 minutes. Beat until soft peaks form.

MAKES 30

Unfilled pastry cones can be made a day ahead.

Storage Airtight container
Freeze Unfilled pastry cones suitable
Microwave Not suitable

APRICOT COCONUT TRIANGLES

8 sheets fillo pastry
90g butter, melted
$^2/_3$ cup (60g) coconut

FILLING
1 cup (150g) dried apricots
$^1/_2$ cup (80g) blanched almonds
1 teaspoon grated lemon rind
1 tablespoon caster sugar
$^1/_4$ cup (60ml) coconut milk

Brush 1 pastry sheet with butter, sprinkle with 1 tablespoon of coconut; cut pastry sheet into 4 strips lengthways. Place 2 level teaspoons of filling at 1 end of each strip.

Fold 1 corner of pastry diagonally across filling to other end to form a triangle. Continue folding to end of strip, retaining triangular shape. Brush with a little more butter. Repeat with remaining pastry, butter, coconut and filling. Place triangles on oven tray, bake in hot oven about 10 minutes or until lightly browned and crisp, serve warm dusted with sifted icing sugar, if desired.

Filling Place apricots in heatproof bowl, cover with boiling water, stand until water is warm; drain. Process apricots and nuts until nuts are chopped. Combine apricot mixture with remaining ingredients in bowl; mix well.

MAKES 32

Recipe can be made 2 days ahead.

Storage Covered, in refrigerator
Freeze Uncooked triangles suitable
Microwave Not suitable

PECAN FUDGE SQUARES

1 quantity basic shortcrust pastry; recipe page 112
$^1/_2$ teaspoon mixed spice

PECAN FILLING
1$^1/_2$ cups (300g) firmly packed brown sugar
$^1/_4$ cup (55g) caster sugar
250g butter
3 cups (375g) chopped pecans
$^1/_4$ cup (60ml) thickened cream

Grease 19cm x 29cm rectangular slab pan, place strip of baking paper to cover base and extend over 2 opposite sides. Make pastry according to directions on page 112. Roll pastry on floured surface sprinkled with spice until large enough to line prepared pan. Lift pastry into pan, ease into side, trim edge. Lightly prick base with fork, refrigerate 30 minutes.

Spoon hot filling into pastry case. Bake in hot oven 25 minutes or until pastry is browned; cool in pan, refrigerate overnight. Dust with sifted icing sugar, if desired.

Pecan Filling Combine sugars and butter in pan, stir over heat, without boiling, until sugar is dissolved. Bring to boil, simmer about 5 minutes, without stirring, or until thickened. Remove from heat, stir in nuts and cream.

MAKES ABOUT 26

Recipe can be made 3 days ahead.

Storage Covered, in refrigerator
Freeze Uncooked pastry suitable
Microwave Not suitable

LEMON RICOTTA TARTLETS

1 quantity basic pate sucree; recipe page 113
¹/₄ cup (55g) caster sugar
1 egg
1 egg yolk
1 teaspoon plain flour
1 teaspoon grated lemon rind
¹/₄ cup (60ml) cream
²/₃ cup (135g) ricotta cheese

Make pastry according to directions on page 113. Roll pastry between sheets of lightly floured baking paper until 2mm thick. Place 11cm boat-shaped tartlet tins 1cm apart, face down on pastry. Cut around tins, leaving 5mm border. Gently press pastry into tins, trim edges, prick lightly with fork, place on oven tray, refrigerate 30 minutes.

Combine sugar, egg, egg yolk, flour and rind in small bowl of electric mixer. Beat about 5 minutes or until thick and pale in colour. Add combined cream and cheese, beat on low speed until smooth.

Place 1 level tablespoon of cheese mixture into each pastry case. Bake in hot oven about 15 minutes or until puffed and lightly browned; cool. Serve dusted with sifted icing sugar, if desired.

MAKES ABOUT 20

Recipe can be made 2 days ahead.

Storage Covered, in refrigerator
Freeze Uncooked pastry suitable
Microwave Not suitable

Far left Apricot coconut triangles
Left Pecan fudge squares
Above Lemon ricotta tartlets

MINI ECCLES CAKES

3 sheets ready-rolled puff pastry
1 egg yolk
caster sugar

FILLING
30g butter
3/4 cup (105g) dried currants
1/4 cup (40g) mixed peel
2 tablespoons caster sugar
1/2 teaspoon ground nutmeg
1/2 teaspoon ground cinnamon

Cut pastry into 12 x 11cm rounds. Place a level tablespoon of filling in centre of each round. Pinch edges together to enclose filling. Turn smooth side up onto lightly floured surface, flatten gently with rolling pin so currants just show through pastry. Shape into ovals, place on greased oven tray. Brush with egg yolk, sprinkle lightly with sugar, cut 3 small slits in top of each oval. Bake in moderately hot oven about 15 minutes or until browned.

Filling Combine butter, fruit, sugar and spices in pan, stir over low heat until butter is melted; cool.

MAKES 12
Recipe can be made 2 days ahead.

Storage Airtight container
Freeze Suitable
Microwave Filling suitable

Tips and techniques

All pastry should be made in cool conditions, and butter and water chilled, unless stated otherwise.

Do not over-handle

When kneading and rolling pastry, handle quickly and lightly, and as little as possible. Heavy handling develops the gluten (protein) in the flour and toughens the pastry. Also, if the butter gets too soft it will be absorbed by the flour, resulting in a crust that is heavy and tough. Avoid re-rolling pastry scraps more than twice; pastry toughens each time it is rolled.

Kneading

Kneading really means turning the outside edges of a dough into the centre. When applied to most pastries it is not strictly kneading, just lightly working the dough into a manageable shape.

Resting

Always "rest" pastry, wrapped in plastic, in the refrigerator for up to 30 minutes before and after rolling. This relaxes the gluten (protein) in the flour and helps avoid shrinkage during baking.

Rolling

Roll pastry evenly on a lightly floured surface or between sheets of baking paper, greaseproof paper or plastic wrap. Start rolling from the centre, outwards, each time, rolling the pastry towards you and away from you. This is vital for pastries such as Puff, Rough Puff and Flaky, where layers are being formed. Reduce the pressure towards the edges; do not roll over the edges.

If rolling on a surface such as timber, marble, etc., keep turning the pastry to ensure it is not stuck to the surface. Use only enough flour to prevent dough sticking; excess flour upsets the balance of the ingredients. Pastry is best rolled on a cold surface; marble is perfect, but use what you've got! Short, light strokes with the rolling pin will give best results.

Lining a dish

Place pastry over rolling pin and carefully lift pastry into the flan tin, pie plate or dish. Gently ease pastry into tin, taking care not to stretch the pastry. Gently push and ease the pastry over the base and side, pressing gently against the surface of the tin to avoid air pockets.

Trimming pastry in a pie plate

Holding the pie plate flat on 1 hand, use a knife to cut away the excess pastry with short, downward strokes; cut away from yourself. Do not drag or stretch the pastry.

Trimming pastry in a flan tin

Using a rolling pin, roll over the flan tin to trim the pastry edge evenly.

Baking pastry cases

1 Cut a sheet of baking paper about 5cm larger than flan tin, pie plate or dish. Cover pastry with paper, fill with dried beans or rice, place on oven tray. Bake in moderately hot oven 10 minutes or as specified.

2 Remove paper and beans carefully from pastry case, bake further 10 minutes or until golden; cool. When beans or rice are cold, store them in an airtight container for future use for baking blind, as this procedure is called.

Storing and freezing

Pastry can be stored, wrapped securely in plastic, in the refrigerator for 1 to 2 days, or frozen for about 2 months.

Double edges

We use 2 types of double edges. These edges are useful when pastry cases have to withstand further baking with a filling. Single-edged crusts will become over-cooked after about 30 minutes.

1 Cut a strip of pastry as wide as the rim of the pie plate. Brush a little water on the rim, then gently press pastry strip onto the rim. Lift pastry into the plate, then brush the strip of pastry lightly with water or beaten egg before pressing the pastry onto the pastry strip.

2 The alternative type of double edge is a thick one especially suitable for decorative finishes. Line the pie plate with pastry, then, using scissors, cut the pastry about 2cm wider than the rim. Carefully fold the pastry under or over to form a double edge, press gently.

Basic pastry recipes

How to make the basic pastries we have used in the recipes throughout this book.

Shortcrust pastry

Shortcrust is probably the most widely used of all pastries, and is good with sweet or savoury fillings.

1½ cups (225g) plain flour
125g cold butter, chopped
1 egg yolk
3 teaspoons iced water, approximately

1 Sift flour into bowl, rub in butter (or process flour and butter until mixture resembles breadcrumbs).

2 Add egg yolk and enough water to make ingredients cling together (or process until ingredients just come together).

3 Press dough into a ball, knead gently on lightly floured surface until smooth. Wrap in plastic, refrigerate 30 minutes.
  Roll pastry between sheets of baking paper until large enough to line tin/dish/plate. Lift pastry into tin, ease into side, trim edge. Lightly prick pastry base with fork, refrigerate 30 minutes.
  Cover pastry with baking paper, fill with dried beans or rice; place on oven tray. Bake in moderately hot oven 10 minutes. Remove paper and beans carefully from pastry case, bake further 10 minutes or until browned; cool.

Wholemeal pastry

A variation of shortcrust pastry, this pastry has the healthy addition of wholemeal flour.

1 cup (160g) wholemeal plain flour
½ cup (75g) white plain flour
125g cold butter, chopped
2 egg yolks
1 tablespoon iced water, approximately

1 Sift flours into bowl, rub in butter (or process flours and butter until the mixture resembles breadcrumbs).

2 Add egg yolks and enough water to make ingredients cling together (or process until mixture just comes together).

3 Press dough into a ball, knead gently on lightly floured surface until smooth. Wrap in plastic, refrigerate 30 minutes.
  Roll pastry between sheets of baking paper until large enough to line tin/dish/plate. Lift pastry into tin, ease into side, trim edge. Lightly prick pastry base with fork, refrigerate 30 minutes.
  Cover pastry with baking paper, fill with dried beans or rice, place on oven tray. Bake in moderately hot oven 10 minutes. Remove paper and beans carefully from pastry case, bake further 10 minutes or until browned; cool.

HINTS FOR MAKING SHORTCRUST PASTRY, BISCUIT PASTRY AND PATE SUCREE

• Use only enough water to make ingredients cling together; too much water will result in excess shrinkage during baking.

• The food processor makes great shortcrust pastry, but take care not to over-process. Use short, quick bursts of power when blending butter into flour. Use only enough water to make ingredients come together.

• Pastry cases sometimes "puff" or develop air pockets during baking. If you spot this happening, wrap a clean tea-towel into a pad and gently push the centre of the hot pastry case to flatten; continue to cook. Tartlet cases can be pressed gently with the back of a spoon.

Choux pastry

"Choux" is the French word for "cabbage" and the pastry is so named because, when made into puffs, the cooked pastry rises up, fat and round, in the shape of a cabbage.

1 cup (250ml) water
80g butter, chopped
1 cup (150g) plain flour
4 eggs

1 Combine water and butter in pan, bring to boil, stirring, until the butter is melted.

2 Add sifted flour all at once, stir vigorously over heat until mixture leaves side of pan and forms a smooth ball.

3 Transfer mixture to small bowl of electric mixer (or into bowl of food processor). Add eggs 1 at a time, beat on low speed until smooth after each addition; mixture should be glossy. Use as specified in individual recipes.

Biscuit pastry

A popular pastry with a soft, biscuit-like texture, this is used for sweet tarts and pies, etc.

90g butter
1/4 cup (55g) caster sugar
1 egg, lightly beaten
11/4 cups (185g) plain flour
1/4 cup (35g) self-raising flour

1 Have butter at room temperature. Beat butter in small bowl with electric mixer until smooth; butter should not change colour. Add sugar and egg, beat only until combined; do not over-beat.

2 Stir in half the sifted flours with a wooden spoon.

3 Work in remaining flours using fingers. Knead pastry gently on lightly floured surface until smooth; do not over-handle. Wrap in plastic, refrigerate 30 minutes.

Roll pastry between sheets of floured baking paper until large enough to line tin/ dish/plate. Lift pastry into tin, ease into side, trim edge. Lightly prick pastry base with fork, refrigerate 30 minutes.

Cover pastry with baking paper, fill with dried beans or rice, place on oven tray. Bake in moderately hot oven 10 minutes. Remove paper and beans carefully from pastry case, bake further 10 minutes or until browned; cool.

Pate sucree

This is the classic French pastry (the name means "sweet pastry") for making sweet pies and tarts.

1 cup (150g) plain flour
1/4 cup (55g) caster sugar
60g cold butter, chopped
2 egg yolks
2 teaspoons iced water, approximately

1 Sift flour onto bench, make well in centre, place sugar, butter and egg yolks in well.

2 Using fingertips of 1 hand, work sugar, butter and yolks together until well blended. Gradually draw in the flour using other hand; work together until all the flour is incorporated, adding enough water to make ingredients cling together (or combine flour, sugar and butter in processor, process about 30 seconds or until

HINTS FOR MAKING CHOUX PASTRY

• Have all ingredients ready before you begin to make the pastry as speed is important during the mixing.

• Do not leave uncooked choux pastry standing; it is important to cook it straight away to give well-risen puffs.

• Do not let the water boil for longer than necessary while melting butter; it will evaporate and upset the balance of ingredients.

• After cooking choux puffs, use a skewer to pierce a hole in the base of each puff so that hot steam can escape.

• Fill puffs just before serving so the pastry won't soften.

mixture resembles breadcrumbs; add egg yolks and enough water to make ingredients cling together).

3 Press ingredients together to form a ball. Knead gently on lightly floured surface until smooth, cover, refrigerate 30 minutes.

Roll pastry between sheets of floured baking paper until large enough to line tin/ dish/plate. Ease pastry into tin, ease into side, trim edge. Lightly prick pastry base with fork, refrigerate 30 minutes.

Cover pastry with baking paper, fill with dried beans or rice, place on oven tray. Bake in moderately hot oven 10 minutes. Remove paper and beans carefully from pastry case, bake further 10 minutes or until browned; cool.

Puff pastry

Layers are created in a certain order as you roll and fold this pastry, the process gives the "puff" to puff pastry.

500g butter
3¹/₃ cups (500g) plain flour
1¹/₄ cups (310ml) iced
water, approximately

1 Have butter at room temperature. Place butter in bowl with ¹/₄ cup (35g) of the flour, work flour and butter together with 1 hand until combined. Shape butter mixture into a square about 2.5cm thick, cover with plastic; refrigerate while preparing dough.

2 Sift remaining flour into bowl, make well in centre, stir in enough iced water to mix to a firm, pliable dough. It will be necessary to use 1 hand to mix the dough as it becomes too stiff to stir.

3 Turn dough onto lightly floured surface, knead quickly and lightly using minimum flour until dough is smooth; shape into a round. Using a sharp knife, cut a cross on top of dough, about 2.5cm deep.

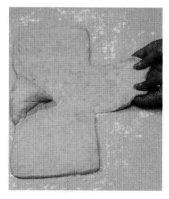

4 Open cross out from centre; gently pull corners out into a 4 leaf clover-shape. Each corner should be large enough to cover the butter square.

5 Place butter square in centre of clover-shape, turn corners over to enclose the butter.

6 Carefully roll dough to about a 25cm x 50cm rectangle. It is important to keep the edges of the dough straight; use a long ruler to pat the sides into shape between rollings. Fold over one-third of the dough, lightly press dough with rolling pin; this helps the next third of dough to fold over neatly. Fold remaining third of dough over. Remember which is the right side up; place dough in plastic bag, refrigerate 30 minutes.

Dough should be cold enough to roll easily (if dough is too cold it will tear and break when rolled; if not cold enough, butter will stick to the bench and rolling pin). For best results, butter and dough should be about the same temperature.

Remove dough from refrigerator, make sure dough is right side up, give dough a quarter turn in 1 direction. (This direction must be continued throughout the rolling process to ensure even layers). Roll again to a rectangle, same size as before, fold again; do this 4 more times, giving a total of 6 folds.

This quantity makes enough puff pastry to cover 2 x 23cm pies.

HINTS FOR MAKING PUFF, ROUGH PUFF AND FLAKY PASTRY

• Rest pastry in refrigerator, in a plastic bag, if it becomes difficult to handle during the rolling and folding. Cool weather is best for pastry making.

• Avoid excessive rolling of dough, this will make the pastry too elastic.

• Roll the dough towards you and away from you, avoiding rolling over the edges; roll to the edge, starting from the centre each time.

• Completed pastry can be refrigerated for up to 2 days or frozen for up to 3 months. Thaw to room temperature before rolling.

• The folding procedures used in puff pastry are similar to rough puff pastry (see Curried Vegetable Jalousie, page 50) and flaky pastry (see Flaky Vegetable Pie, page 54). These 3 pastries are interchangeable.

• Always keep the pastry scraps flat; stack them on top of each other (do not squash into a ball) before rolling. This will help the layers to puff.

• Make sure glaze doesn't run down the sides of pie when glazing the pastry. This can seal the layers, affecting the rise of the pastry.

CHOCOLATE DECORATIONS

Spoon melted Choc Melts into piping bag fitted with small plain tube. Pipe decorative shapes on baking paper. Allow to set at room temperature.

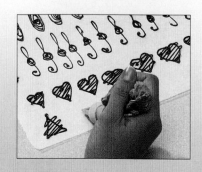

Decorating ideas

Quick and simple ideas to add the finishing touch to your pies and tart.

Crimped edge

Position the thumb and index finger of 1 hand inside the pastry rim, push from the outside to create a crimped edge.

Spoon-scalloped edge

Press an upturned spoon into the pastry to form 1 or more rows of scallops for an extra-easy decoration.

Braided edge

Cut 1cm-wide strips of pastry and braid together. Brush pastry rim with water or lightly beaten egg, place braid on rim; press gently.

Feather edge

Using sharp scissors, snip slanted incisions around the edge of the pastry to give a feathered effect.

Checkerboard edge

Trim pastry so it extends 1cm over edge of plate. Using scissors or a sharp knife, cut at 1cm intervals. Brush edge with water or lightly beaten egg. Fold over every alternate square to give a checkerboard effect.

Shapes

Using small cutters, cut shapes from rolled-out scraps. Brush pastry edge with water or lightly beaten egg, place shapes around edge; press gently. Brush every shape with water or egg before sticking another shape to it.

Leaves

Cut rolled-out scraps into leaf shapes, using a sharp knife; mark in veins. Brush pastry rim with water or lightly beaten egg, place leaves around rim; press gently. Brush every leaf with water or egg before sticking another leaf to it.

Pointed edge

Position the thumb and index finger of 1 hand outside the pastry rim, push from the inside with other index finger to create a pointed edge.

GLOSSARY

ALLSPICE pimento.

APPLE JELLY a clear preserve made from fresh fruit and sugar.

ARBORIO RICE large, round-grained rice especially suitable for risottos.

ARMAGNAC a fine brandy from the Armagnac area in Southern France.

BACON RASHERS also known as slices of bacon.

BLOOD ORANGE very sweet, juicy orange with red colouring on the skin and flesh.

BREADCRUMBS
Packaged fine packaged breadcrumbs.
Stale 1- or 2-day-old bread made into crumbs by grating, blending or processing.

BUTTER use salted or unsalted (also called sweet) butter; 125g is equal to 1 stick butter.

BUTTERMILK low-fat milk, cultured to give slightly sour, tangy taste; low-fat yogurt can be substituted.

CANELLE KNIFE a kitchen utensil used to cut v-shaped grooves into the surface of fruit and vegetables for decorative effect.

CASSIS blackcurrant-flavoured liqueur.

CELERIAC tuberous root with brown skin, white flesh and a celery-like flavour.

CHEESE
Feta a soft Greek cheese with a sharp, salty taste.
Mascarpone a fresh, unripened, smooth triple-cream cheese with a delicately sweet, slightly sour taste.
Mozzarella a semi-soft cheese with a delicate, fresh taste; has a low melting point and stringy texture when it is heated.

CHICKPEAS garbanzos.

CHILLIES are available in many different types and sizes. Use rubber gloves when chopping fresh chillies as they can burn your skin.
Sweet chilli sauce a comparatively mild, Thai-type sauce made from red chillies, sugar, garlic and vinegar.
Chilli powder the Asian variety is the hottest and is made from ground chillies; it can be used as a substitute for fresh chillies in the proportions of 1/2 teaspoon ground chilli powder to 1 medium chopped fresh chilli.

CHOC MELTS discs of dark compounded chocolate ideal for melting and moulding.

CINNAMON SUGAR a combination of sugar and cinnamon available from supermarkets.

COCONUT use desiccated coconut unless otherwise specified.
Cream produced by squeezing the coconut flesh. Available in cans and cartons.
Flaked flaked coconut flesh.
Milk available in cans from supermarkets.
Shredded thin strips of dried coconut.

COINTREAU orange-flavoured liqueur.

CORNFLOUR cornstarch.

CORNMEAL ground corn (maize); similar to polenta but pale yellow and finer. One can be substituted for the other.

CREAM fresh pouring cream; has a minimum fat content of 35 per cent.
Sour a thick, commercially cultured soured cream.
Thickened (whipping) is specified when necessary in recipes. Has a minimum fat content of 35 per cent, with the addition of a thickener.

CREAM OF HORSERADISH paste of horseradish, oil, mustard and flavourings.

CREAM OF TARTAR an acid; when combined with an alkali such as bicarbonate of soda acts as a raising agent. It is one of the ingredients in baking powder.

CREME DE CACAO a chocolate-flavoured liqueur.

CREME FRAICHE available in cartons from delicatessens and supermarkets. To make creme fraiche, combine 300ml cream with 300ml sour cream in bowl, cover, stand at room temperature until mixture is thick; this will take 1 or 2 days, depending on room temperature. Sweeten to taste, if desired. Refrigerate before using. Makes about 21/2 cups (625ml).

CSABAI SALAMI mild smoked salami made from pork, seasoned with cracked peppercorns and paprika.

CUSTARD POWDER vanilla pudding mix.

DRAMBUIE liqueur made from whisky, honey and herbs.

ENGLISH SPINACH a soft-leafed vegetable, more delicate in taste than silverbeet (spinach); young silverbeet can be substituted for English spinach.

FLOUR
White plain unbleached all-purpose flour.
White self-raising substitute plain (all-purpose) flour and baking powder in the proportions of 1 cup (150g) plain flour to 2 level teaspoons baking powder. Sift together several times before using.
Wholemeal plain also known as wholewheat flour without the addition of baking powder.

FRANGELICO hazelnut-flavoured liqueur.

GARAM MASALA this spice combines varying proportions of cardamom, cinnamon, cloves, coriander, fennel and cumin, roasted and ground together. Black pepper and chilli can be added for a hotter version.

GHEE a pure butter fat available in cans or tubs; it can be heated to high temperatures without burning because of the lack of salts and milk solids.

GINGER fresh, green or root ginger; scrape away skin and grate, chop or slice as needed.

GOLDEN SYRUP maple, pancake syrup or honey can be substituted.

GREEN GINGER WINE alcoholic sweet wine infused with finely ground ginger.

GRAND MARNIER an orange-flavoured liqueur.

GREEN PEPPERCORNS available in cans or jars, pickled in brine.

GREEN SHALLOTS also known as scallions, eschallots and green onions. Do not confuse with small French shallots.

HOI SIN SAUCE a thick, sweet and spicy Chinese paste made from salted fermented soy beans, onions and garlic; used as a marinade or baste, or to accent stir-fries and barbecued or roasted foods.

JAM preserve of sugar and fruit.

KAHLUA coffee-flavoured liqueur.

KIRSCH cherry-flavoured liqueur.

KIWI FRUIT also known as Chinese gooseberry.

KUMARA Polynesian name of orange-fleshed sweet potato often confused with yam.

LARD fat obtained by melting down and clarifying pork fat; available packaged.

LEEK a member of the onion family, resembles the green shallot but is much larger.

LIGHT CORN SYRUP an imported product available in supermarkets, delicatessens and health food stores.

MALIBU coconut-flavoured rum-based liquor.

MARSALA sweet, fortified wine.

MIXED PEEL a mixture of crystallised citrus peel; also known as candied peel.

MIXED SPICE a blend of ground spices usually consisting of cinnamon, allspice and nutmeg.

MORTADELLA a delicately spiced and smoked cooked sausage made from pork and beef.

MUSHROOMS
Button small, cultivated white mushrooms with a delicate, subtle flavour.

Cup slightly larger, opened mushrooms.
Flat large, soft, flat mushrooms with a rich earthy flavour.
Oyster (abalone) pale grey-white mushrooms, shaped like a fan.
Swiss brown light to dark brown mushrooms with full-bodied flavour. Button or cup mushrooms can be substituted for Swiss browns.

OLIVE PASTE also known as olive pate, is made from olives, olive oil, salt, vinegar and herbs.

PARSLEY, FLAT-LEAFED also known as continental parsley or Italian parsley.

PASTRY
Fillo frozen wafer-thin sheets of pastry.
Frozen puff pastry block frozen unbaked 375g block of puff pastry.
Ready-rolled butter puff pastry frozen sheets of puff pastry.
Ready-rolled puff pastry frozen sheets of puff pastry.
Ready-rolled puff pastry roll a frozen sheet of rolled puff pastry. Available in 500g packets. Thaw before unrolling.
Ready-rolled shortcrust pastry frozen sheets of shortcrust pastry.

PEPPERS capsicum or bell peppers.

PEPPERONI sausage made from pork and beef; flavoured with hot red pepper.

PIMIENTOS canned or bottled peppers.

PINE NUT also known as pignoli; small, cream-coloured soft kernels obtained from the cones of different varieties of pine trees.

PLUM SAUCE a dipping sauce made from plums, sugar, chillies and spices.

POLENTA a flour-like cereal made of ground corn (maize); similar to cornmeal but coarser and darker in colour. Also the name of the dish made from it.

PRAWNS also called shrimp.

PROSCIUTTO salted-cured, air-dried (unsmoked), pressed ham; sold ready to eat.

REDCURRANT JELLY a preserve made from redcurrants used as a glaze for desserts and meats or in sauces.

RED SPANISH ONION large, purplish-red onion.

RHUBARB a vegetable, however, the stalks are cooked and eaten as a fruit.

ROCKET also arugula and rugala; a green salad leaf.

ROSEWATER extract made from crushed rose petals.

ROSE PETALS cut fresh rose petals after the dew has disappeared and before the sun gets hot. Petals then have the most fragrance and flavour. Choose undamaged petals, free from blemishes do not use roses treated with insecticide or pesticide.

SAFFRON dried crocus stigmas available in strands or powder form; the quality varies greatly.

Strands have an aromatic, slightly bitter taste, and only a few are required to flavour and colour dishes.
Powder the flavour is not the same as strands; only a pinch is needed to colour dishes. Turmeric can be substituted.

OELEK (also ulek or olek) a paste made from ground chillies and salt.

SALT, COARSE COOKING a coarse salt (not the same as fine table salt).

SEASONED PEPPER a combination of black pepper, sugar and bell pepper.

SEMOLINA a hard part of the wheat which is sifted out; used mainly for making pasta.

SILVERBEET steam green leafy parts and use as required in recipes.

STAR ANISE a dried star-shaped pod whose seeds have an astringent aniseed flavour. Used mainly in Asian recipes.

STOCK 1 cup (250ml) stock is the equivalent of 1 cup (250ml) water plus 1 crumbled stock cube (or 1 teaspoon stock powder).

SUGAR we used coarse granulated table sugar, also known as crystal sugar, unless otherwise specified.
Brown an extremely soft, fine granulated sugar retaining molasses for its characteristic deep colour and flavour.
Caster also known as superfine or finely granulated table sugar.
Icing sugar mixture also known as confectioners' sugar or powdered sugar; granulated sugar crushed together with a small amount (about 3%) of cornflour added.
Palm very fine sugar from the coconut palm. It is usually sold in compressed cakes. Also known as *gula jawa*, *melaka* and *jaggery*. Palm sugar can be substituted with brown or black sugar.

SULTANAS seedless white raisins.

TABASCO SAUCE made with vinegar, hot red peppers and salt. Use sparingly in drops.

VANILLA BEAN dried bean of the vanilla orchid. It can be used repeatedly; simply wash in warm water after use, dry well and store in airtight container.

VANILLA ESSENCE also known as extract; we used imitation vanilla essence.

WHITE MELTS discs of compounded white chocolate ideal for melting and moulding.

WITLOF also known as chicory or Belgian endive.

YEAST a 7g ($^{1}/_{4}$oz) sachet of dried yeast (2 teaspoons) is equal to 15g ($^{1}/_{2}$oz) compressed yeast if substituting 1 for the other.

ZUCCHINI also known as courgette.

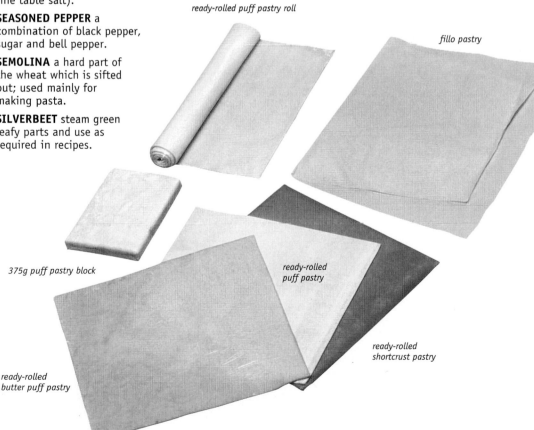

ready-rolled puff pastry roll

fillo pastry

375g puff pastry block

ready-rolled puff pastry

ready-rolled shortcrust pastry

ready-rolled butter puff pastry

INDEX

MAKE YOUR OWN STOCK

These recipes can be made up to 4 days ahead and stored, covered, in the refrigerator. Be sure to remove any fat from the surface after the cooled stock has been refrigerated overnight. If the stock is to be kept longer, it is best to freeze it in smaller quantities.

Stock is also available in cans or tetra packs. Stock cubes or powder can be used. As a guide, 1 teaspoon of stock powder or 1 small crumbled stock cube mixed with 1 cup (250ml) water will give a fairly strong stock. Be aware of the salt and fat content of stock cubes and powders and prepared stocks.

All stock recipes make about 2.5 litres (10 cups).

BEEF STOCK

2kg meaty beef bones
2 medium (300g) onions
2 sticks celery, chopped
2 medium (250g) carrots, chopped
3 bay leaves
2 teaspoons black peppercorns
5 litres (20 cups) water
3 litres (12 cups) water, extra

Place bones and unpeeled chopped onions in baking dish. Bake in hot oven about 1 hour or until bones and onions are well browned. Transfer bones and onions to large pan, add celery, carrots, bay leaves, peppercorns and water, simmer, uncovered, 3 hours. Add extra water, simmer, uncovered, further 1 hour; strain.

CHICKEN STOCK

2kg chicken bones
2 medium (300g) onions, chopped
2 sticks celery, chopped
2 medium (250g) carrots, chopped
3 bay leaves
2 teaspoons black peppercorns
5 litres (20 cups) water

Combine all ingredients in large pan, simmer, uncovered, 2 hours; strain.

FISH STOCK

1.5kg fish bones
3 litres (12 cups) water
1 medium (150g) onion, chopped
2 sticks celery, chopped
2 bay leaves
1 teaspoon black peppercorns

Combine all ingredients in large pan, simmer, uncovered, 20 minutes; strain.

VEGETABLE STOCK

2 large (360g) carrots, chopped
2 large (360g) parsnips, chopped
4 medium (600g) onions, chopped
12 sticks celery, chopped
4 bay leaves
2 teaspoons black peppercorns
6 litres (24 cups) water

Combine all ingredients in large pan, simmer, uncovered, 1½ hours; strain.

FACTS AND FIGURES

Wherever you live, you'll be able to use our recipes with the help of these easy-to-follow conversions. While these conversions are approximate only, the difference between an exact and the approximate conversion of various liquid and dry measures is but minimal and will not affect your cooking results.

DRY MEASURES

Metric	Imperial
15g	1/2oz
30g	1oz
60g	2oz
90g	3oz
125g	4oz (1/4lb)
155g	5oz
185g	6oz
220g	7oz
250g	8oz (1/2lb)
280g	9oz
315g	10oz
345g	11oz
375g	12oz (3/4lb)
410g	13oz
440g	14oz
470g	15oz
500g	16oz (1lb)
750g	24oz (11/2lb)
1kg	32oz (2lb)

LIQUID MEASURES

Metric	Imperial
30ml	1 fluid oz
60ml	2 fluid oz
100ml	3 fluid oz
125ml	4 fluid oz
150ml	5 fluid oz (1/4 pint/1 gill)
190ml	6 fluid oz
250ml	8 fluid oz
300ml	10 fluid oz (1/2 pint)
500ml	16 fluid oz
600ml	20 fluid oz (1 pint)
1000ml (1 litre)	13/4 pints

HELPFUL MEASURES

Metric	Imperial
3mm	1/8in
6mm	1/4in
1cm	1/2in
2cm	3/4in
2.5cm	1in
5cm	2in
6cm	21/2in
8cm	3in
10cm	4in
13cm	5in
15cm	6in
18cm	7in
20cm	8in
23cm	9in
25cm	10in
28cm	11in
30cm	12in (1ft)

MEASURING EQUIPMENT

The difference between one country's measuring cups and another's is, at most, within a 2 or 3 teaspoon variance. (For the record, 1 Australian metric measuring cup holds approximately 250ml.) The most accurate way of measuring dry ingredients is to weigh them. When measuring liquids, use a clear glass or plastic jug with the metric markings.

Note: North America and UK use 15ml tablespoons. Australian tablespoons measure 20ml. All cup and spoon measurements are level.

How To Measure

When using graduated metric measuring cups, shake dry ingredients loosely into the appropriate cup. Do not tap the cup on a bench or tightly pack the ingredients unless directed to do so. Level top of measuring cups and measuring spoons with a knife. When measuring liquids, place a clear glass or plastic jug with metric markings on a flat surface to check accuracy at eye level.

We use large eggs having an average weight of 60g.

OVEN TEMPERATURES

These oven temperatures are only a guide. Always check the manufacturer's manual.

	C° (Celsius)	F° (Fahrenheit)	Gas Mark
Very slow	120	250	1
Slow	150	300	2
Moderately slow	160	325	3
Moderate	180 - 190	350 - 375	4
Moderately hot	200 - 210	400 - 425	5
Hot	220 - 230	450 - 475	6
Very hot	240 - 250	500 - 525	7